# SUMMERS WITH MEMERE

## BY
## MARIE SHARPE SCHNERCH

Order this book online at www.trafford.com
or email orders@trafford.com

Most Trafford titles are also available at major online book retailers.

Print information available on the last page.

ISBN: 978-1-4120-9389-7 (sc)

*Trafford rev. 05/06/2020*

 www.trafford.com

**North America & international**
toll-free: 1 888 232 4444 (USA & Canada)
fax: 812 355 4082

# L'AVE MARIA

Je vous salue, Marie, pleine de grace, le Seigneur est avec vous; vous etes benie entre toutes les femmes et Jesus, le fruit de vos entrailles, est beni. Sainte Marie, Mere de Dieu, priez pour nous, pauvres pecheurs, maintenant et a l'heure de notre mort. Ainsi soit-il.

My Mom, the former, Petersfield "Mrs. Washup"

DEDICATED TO
ELIZABETH ALBINA (ROY) SHARPE
my mother

# TABLE OF CONTENTS

# SUMMERS WITH MEMERE

Petersfield, Manitoba, in the 1950's and 60's was a small village barely sitting on the lip of highway number 9 which stretched north to other places like Winnipeg Beach and Gimli. Dusty gravel roads spider-legged from the small town, some returning farmers home from Sunday church services and Veitch's country store or from trips into Winnipeg and other surrounding hamlets and villages where the business of land owners was conducted. Other rutted lanes hugged the shores of Netley Creek with its lush trees and reedy vegetation bending to the green, reflecting water, which eventually meandered through a marshland channel and emptied into Lake Winnipeg. These roads were dotted with a few summer cabins and resort areas that welcomed vacationing city-dwellers with a peacefulness seldom found so near a big city.

It was back in those days, I spent three or four summer weeks each year on a waterfront lot in Petersfield, with Memere, Mom, my brother Andre, Auntie Emma and her three kids. Auntie Emma, Uncle Tommy and Mom were the beneficiaries of the property and no one wanted the place to sit idle. Memere strongly suggested the clean air and sunshine would bring us all up to snuff, mentally and physically, after the long cold Winnipeg city winters.

My Memere was of French and Irish decent, a rather

short woman, a bit on the plump side with unblemished child-like hands and straight round ankle-less legs. Adelina Roy was her name but I was taught to call her Memere as soon as words began to form in my mouth. Born in the late 1800's, she would survive to live ninety-one years, witnessing the mid-western Canadian landscape transform from limitless unencumbered prairies to fenced acreage and crowded city centers stretching to urban sprawl.

While in her seventies, her silvery-gray hair, always full with tightly permed curls, occasionally glowed with a purplish hue or a steely blue tint. Not needing much nourishment to fuel her aged body, she ate just small bites from refrigerator leftovers or cold supper sandwiches and seldom slept, only when the "sandman" caught her sitting still in the afternoons or in the wee hours of the morning. When she laughed, it seemed like a stifled effort to camouflage a private joke and although we knew she had a strong sense of family, she seldom demonstrated any kind of affection except when presenting her cheek for a kiss at the Christmas Reveillon. Her greatest loyalties would lay with her God and she worked tirelessly to aid in the upkeep of the church and the survival of her faith. She made deals with The Almighty, his angels and the saints as she did with most of her business associates and even her family. Her ways seemed domineering to her children as she hovered a little too close, trying her best to carry weight when it came to their health, financial interests and the molding of her grandchildren. Her voice would ring in our phone at least three or four times a day asking personal questions without any embarrassment and confidently offering sage advice which she expected us all to accept without question. The only one to openly reject her expectations was my father. His stubbornness equaled hers but only served to give her a respect for this

Englishman who married her youngest child and made a home for her on his own terms.

Despite the years that instilled arthritis and ailments that come with advanced age, her mind remained bright and restless till her demise one cold February evening in 1977.

As I remember in the late 1950's, Memere and my Uncle Tommy owned and managed the Roblin, a men's hotel in the inner city. The establishment was erected in the mid 1800's in an area, which was then the hub of civilized activity in Winnipeg. A modest three stories in height, the second and third floor consisted mostly of single rooms for rent along with a few austere communal bathrooms and the main level housed a beer parlor, the walls veneered in highly lacquered stripped logs. A long polished bar, based with a brass footrest and shiny, squat, spittoons hugged one wall, as the rest of the rectangular room was a jumble of chrome chairs sporting vinyl seat covers huddled around small square tables. Grandpa Lauzon, Memere's father, who first owned the place around 1895, would sometimes vault over the bar, gun in hand to break up brawls and liquor- induced disputes between the ever-present patrons. Later, under Memere and Uncle Tommy's management, quiet daytime streets, tall gray storage buildings and drab factories surrounded the hotel and a mortuary occupied a slot directly across the street. Nights were filled with sounds of footsteps echoing in the long hallways, the muted voices of late evening stragglers and the low rumblings of trains sneaking into the darkened city by the tracks along the hotel's narrow back alley.

The Roblin was inhabited by a collection of colorful old buzzards, most sporting wrinkles and gray hair from life's past adventures. Many were veterans, suffering from disabilities of body as well as mind and most were down on their luck. Problems were sometimes lost in the golden bottoms of ten-cent glasses of cold beer and there was always safety in their rooms, up the grand staircase and down the green and yellow, diamond patterned linoleum hallways. They rested weary minds in antique beds and faced themselves in mirrors of gentleman's washstands, fashioned long before the turn of the last century.

The sharp cornered, double faced, brick and stucco front of the building showcased a large vestibule, which was opened to all who passed, by three plate glass windows. Bold wooden armchairs lined the walls and accompanied a battered heavy rectangular table, set to one side of the cavernous room. Sunday nights, Memere could often be found there, playing cards with some of the old guys, a green visor protruding from her forehead. Moth-eaten moose-heads with poker faces would peek from the walls, down over the shoulders of the little group of gamblers as they often played late into the night. Tales of bravery were boasted, great debates decided upon and pittances were won and lost around the old table on those historically small nights. As with all things, times change, most of the old soldiers moved on, some in death and others to nursing homes and the hotel which was once Memere's pride is now only a parking lot.

Memere and my grandfather, Origene Roy, were separated before Mom was born. I never witnessed them standing side by side or ever even having been in the same place at one time. I cannot imagine what brought them so close as to marry, knowing their personalities must have been as different as the sun and moon. He was a hunting guide and horseman, a man whose roots were as old as the land and she, a woman of structure and business, preferring the city sidewalks to country roads and wild marshy trails. He was a romantic and she, wasted nothing on such frill, making her thoughts known to us all in speeches concerning modesty

12

and what should take place only in the "boudoir."

Pepere continued to live on the ranch in St. Ambrose, Manitoba, after Memere gathered their children and relocated to Winnipeg in 1919. Pepere was introduced to dignitaries from home and abroad, guiding them in hunting and fishing and entertaining the guests at his rustic lodge in the Delta Marsh. As his aging body sapped his energies and became a hindrance to his work, he semi-retired and in 1948 moved to Petersfield, the small town situated about forty miles north of Winnipeg. The small town I will tell you about.

The house was not wired for electricity so my father, who worked for the hydro company, scrounged some equipment and found a colleague to do the work. The glow from 25-watt bulbs warmed the atmosphere of the approaching coolness of country nights and a big wooden crank style, party line phone was installed on one of the living-room walls. Although his age was far from that of the hale young man who once rode horseback though miles of high grasses in the Delta Marsh, Pepere was again ready to settle in and welcome the odd fisherman and autumn hunter.

His new home was a six- bedroom, story and a half insilbrick house settled to one side of about one quarter acre of land along the banks of the scenic Netley Creek. An old wooden shingle, with "OROY" painted in white, was nailed to the gate should someone not know who resided there. The lot also supported a lush orchard of fruit trees, a large garden and dilapidated old barn. Pepere's house was crammed with dusty old over-stuffed furniture and the walls were covered with hunting pictures from days of yore. I especially remember the substantial oil paintings of sheep filled valleys and stark mountain peaks framed in ornate golden curls and colorfully headed stuffed ducks sitting permanently motionless atop the treadle sewing machine and old, rickety corner table. Crude duck and goose decoys found a new home in the front hall closet along with fishing rods, two old shot-guns and some paddles belonging to the green and red canoes laying idle in the barn. Two of the walk-in bedroom closets housed chamber pots and white enameled jugs with matching washbowls chipped black from years of not so gentle use.

In 1951, Pepere suffered a massive heart attack and died after spending one cool afternoon endeavoring to chop down a dead tree on the property. His body was brought to the city where after viewing and an elaborate funeral mass, it was laid to rest in the ground of an urban Catholic cemetery.

Few things were changed in his house after his passing, if not for the film of gray dust covering the furniture and warm empty refrigerator, one would think he were still there, just gone fishing.

We didn't own a car so Uncle Tommy drove us from Winnipeg to Petersfield for our summer holidays, in his 1957 two-toned green Oldsmobile. On the appointed Sunday morning, he would arrive with Memere to pick up Mom, Andre and me, along with a months supply of food and every medical remedy usually residing in our bathroom medicine cabinet. Mom firmly believed in being prepared for everything short of the sky coming apart. We called it her medicine chest, but it was really just an old suitcase stuffed with remedies such as bottles of aspirin, St. Joseph's oil sent all the way from Montreal, rubbing alcohol for disinfecting things like the outhouse seat and brown bottles of peroxide for treatment of "serious wounds". The glass bottles were kept from clinking by wads of bandages, cotton batting and a months supply of Kotex.

There was no running water at the house so we brought

our own water filled javex jugs, which anchored the car as it labored away from the curb. Memere always sat in the front passenger seat and Mom, Andre and I in the back, usually with a 20-pound watermelon or a hired man from the hotel. It was always a different fellow Uncle Tommy brought each time to help with digging the gardens and slapping a bit of paint on the old barn. I expect it was an opportunity for the old guys to work off room rent or a bar tab. Sometimes they reeked of beer or body odor and cigarettes. We just opened the back windows a crack and held our noses high as the roar of the wind pushing through the cracks rendered us deaf by the time we reached our destination. We looked forward to the car finally turning right onto the dusty gravel road, past the small white church on the corner. There came a couple more right turns, past Trossi's turkey farm with the big red barn, then a left before we pulled into the overgrown yard. Auntie Emma and her kids were always there before our arrival. Auntie's boyfriend, Nick usually drove them down the day before in his old panel truck.

The first thing Memere did after stepping from the car was to head straight to the barn and dust off her lawn mower. She'd have the hired man fill it with gas and then she would lay slaughter to any greenery in her path. Long emerald carpet-like strips emerged from the tall waving sea of spring grass, stretching from the road to the uneven banks of the creek, as morning turned into afternoon. I think this exercise was Memere's best excuse to spend all her time outside inhaling the beauty of nature, because her life at home was almost completely surrounded by the gray cement, bricks and mortar of the city's core.

Sometimes Nick stayed on a couple of days, but usually the men left on Sunday evenings after a country barbecue feast, served in the small screened-in porch attached to the east side of the house. A long table occupied most of the floor space with a narrow bench on each side and two chairs, one at each end of the table for Memere and sometimes my Dad. Everyone would be practically sitting on each other in a sticky clump, all of them reaching for the same thing at the same time. It was amazing how quickly the kitchen would be organized enough to serve such an elaborate meal, not to mention Auntie's fresh baked butterscotch meringue pies. Memere, our matriarch, would sit in her chair, overseeing the culinary event with an air of power exhibiting a gleam in her eye that let us know we would be at her mercy for the next couple of weeks.

The evening always brought a kind of settling. Everyone slowly began adjusting to the lack of modern comforts but at the same time, grew to appreciate the quietness and natural beauty surrounding us. The setting sun transformed our country horizons to a bright copper, red and gold, even on cloudless skies and held the night at bay till everyone had their fill of such glorious sights. We would fall drowsy from country air into our beds, which still seemed to hold the winter dampness, taking the warmth from our bodies and giving back a kind of clamminess. It was so black and silent on moonless nights after the others were asleep I felt I could hardly breathe. Mom sometimes left the light on in the closet and the door open a bit in case we needed to use the chamber pot. The only thing I really missed during those days at Petersfield was our sweet-smelling bathroom at home and our toilet with the visible white bottom. There was something eerie about hanging my posterior above a deep, black hole in which I believed any wild animal could hide undetected, only to jump up and take a bite out of unsuspecting squatters.

Early mornings greeted us with the drone of Memere's lawn mower and the smell of exhaust hanging over the yard. Mom and Auntie Emma could usually be found cleaning the winter hue from the house, replacing it with sparkling floors, clean carpets and the aromas of fried bacon, toast and fresh coffee. It would take a good couple of days before the house was cleaned and disinfected to satisfy Mom's standards.

My brother, three cousins and I were expected to rake the grass clippings from Memere's incessant mowing. Sometimes we worked together in shifts and sometimes alone depending how many rakes could be found. Cousin Phil was a master at losing rakes or any tool he thought might interfere with his leisure activity time. Stacks of grass clippings dotted the property at the end of each day as Memere stood over her domain openly gleeful at the sight. She would set fire to the mounds we had gathered, seemingly taking great satisfaction in watching the still moist grass spew clouds of gray smoke across the yard and creek. Not an evening went by that there wasn't a ribbon of white rising to join the blanket of haze covering our property. It's a wonder we didn't all suffer from some kind of pulmonary disease. At best, we always smelled a little burnt.

Memere, being a businesswoman, paid us for our time. She brought large cartons containing shiny boxes of Black Magic chocolates and bags of potato chips from the hotel. I now realize the confections had long outlived their "best by" dates and she was determined to get her worth from them. In the evenings after supper, when everyone was nursing the days bug bites and sunburns, Memere would determine our wages and dole out the stale, white coated chocolates accordingly.

Despite any precautions Mom took, horse flies always bit Andre and me. They were huge, multi-colored flies possessed with a passion for tender young ankles. Our feet swelled to an obscene size and itched unmercifully. Mom would finally abandon her medicine chest and resort to tying a large pork rind around my ankle, which resembled a pink grapefruit with digits. Mom's grandfather, who was a butcher, told her about this remedy many years ago. When I was finished with the pork rind, Auntie Emma put it in an aluminum pan and placed it in the oven. After about ten minutes of listening to it crackle and snap in the heat, she would remove the rind, break it into bite size pieces, sprinkle a little salt and step back while we all jumped for the first crunchy taste. We never learned to wait till it cooled, burning our tongues to tastelessness for the next couple of hours.

One leisure activity I enjoyed immensely was fishing. There was a big patch of yellow flowered lily pads just about sixty feet from the old gray floating dock. We spent hours pulling little mud pouts and perch from beneath the murky surface of the water just beyond the lily patch. Auntie Emma and Memere loved to sit at one end of the dock soaking the calluses on the bottoms of their feet in the coolness of the creek. One day, Auntie mentioned to Nick that she would like to see one of those lilies up close and smell its perfume. Being a man in love, he immediately stripped to his trunks and swam out to fulfill her request. Returning to the dock, he pulled himself up in a gush of green water and presented her with an odorous golden bloom atop a thirteen-foot stem. Even in my adolescence, I thought it quite romantic. Nick would eventually be recruited to weed a path through the flat, green leaves to make way for the boat to pass, saving the motor from choking. He spent many hours under water, holding his breath for what seemed endless minutes at a time, emerging with long pale green tendrils in his strong huge hands. The gap to the wide clear creek still exists to this day.

My cousin Yvonne and I used to escape in the motorboat as soon as cousins Phil and Victor returned from the channel with their morning catch. They usually set out about seven a.m., so by ten we were waiting impatiently on the dock, straining our ears, hoping to hear the buzz of the little motor rounding the bend to the creek. Yvonne was always her usual fetching self in a straw hat, shorts and of course, a big black over-blown inner tube around her waist for safety. Most times the motor died and we'd be reduced to using the oars. Yvonne would recite Hail Marys all the way back to the dock, just in case we should encounter any more perils on the mighty Netley Creek. Despite our bad luck and inexperience with motors, we continued to go out in the boat whenever we got the chance figuring the paddling was a good exercise for the development of a womanly chest.

We said numerous Hail Marys at Petersfield. Memere, a devout Roman Catholic, demanded our presence every evening for a fifteen-minute recitation of the rosary along with CKSB, the French radio station. Come 6:45 p.m. we would hear our names being called, echoing in the evening stillness across the creek and into all the corners of the property. This obligation was not to be ignored because "God was watching." I don't understand much French. It seemed like an eternity, kneeling for a quarter of an hour listening to French, all the while leaning on a big musty chair, which had been home to mice all winter.

Sunday morning Mass was an experience in itself. Nick usually spent the weekends with us and provided our transportation to church. He owned a milky sea green colored two-door delivery van. There were cargo doors at the very back with two windows and   nothing to hang on to inside the truck, just slick bare walls and floor. Nick drove with Auntie and Memere squeezed beside him on the grease stained bench seat as Mom joined us kids in the back, to be bounced and jostled for ten minutes along the bumpy gravel road. Upon our arrival at St. Annes Catholic Church, the locals would stare in amazement as Nick promptly opened the back doors and we tumbled out, not unlike the little car full of clowns you might see at the circus. We would straighten up; press the crinkles from our clothes with the palms of our hands and proudly file into church. The bell rang out as the service started but half way through mass, the seats became harder, the air warmer and the choir a source of giggles and face making. Memere always sat behind us kids so as to keep us settled with a few sharp pokes and a bop on the head with her prayer book. Occasionally she would sing along with the exuberant little choir as they belted out "Oh Jesus Heart all Burning" in crescendos from their station beside the simple organ situated at the back of the church.

We were all living under each other's feet despite the expanse of land with its quiet corners in the leafy orchard and musty cool barn. Tempers flared at times. Auntie Emma and Memere were both strong personalities and I could hear them grating on each other some nights after we kids were in bed. My cousins, brother and I also had our share of spats and squabbles; mostly over who was cheating at cards or whose turn it was at bat. All in all, we shared the space quite well, had wonderful times and lots of laughs.

We learned many important things from those summers with Memere. We learned that old people can still outsmart young people, bacon rinds do not reduce swelling and Netley Creek water lilies smell atrocious.

I think the most important thing I learned was, hard work and a job well done should be performed as a source of personal pride, because sometimes the only tangible reward is a stale chocolate.

Memere

# MRS. WASH-UP
# AND
# THE GREAT MEDICINE CHEST

My Mom was affectionately known as "Mrs. Wash-up" by Auntie Emma, her kids and Memere when we took our annual holidays in Petersfield.

Her proper name is Elizabeth, but friends and family have always called her Betty. The last child born to Memere, her entrance in 1919 coincided with other historic events such as the great Winnipeg labor strike, global flu epidemic and the lifting of the Golden Boy statue to the apex of the Manitoba parliament buildings.

A puny looking little thing, she was coaxed and prodded by her elders to eat and spend more time in the sun. They had no idea of the strength that lived within her mind and body and would surely gather momentum with maturity.

Mother was raised by her maternal grandparents in the ancestral home; a large green trimmed white house located in the North end of Winnipeg. It was conspicuously perched on the top of a rise which ever so slowly leveled to the rugged banks of the muddy Red River. Her childhood and adolescence were carefree and happy, despite the absence of both her parents. Many summer hours were whiled away daydreaming in the lush green yard with its towering elms and sweeping maple trees or sitting on the wrap-around veranda with Grandma and Grandpa Lauzon, indulging in bowls of frosty Neapolitan ice cream. Her Grandpa's elaborate stories recited in his thick, French accent would remain in her memories to this day along with the strong sense of duty and compassion instilled in her soul by her Irish-French Grandmother's example. Mother grew into adulthood, gifted with an independent mind and a stubborn will, camouflaged by a genuine kindness of heart and fluid generosity.

Memere was occupied with business ventures, earning a living for her family and had little time for basic childcare. As the years turned Mom into a woman, she and Memere would become so close there would be few secrets.

Mom met my dad, Harry at a Sacred Heart church whist drive in 1935. Money was scarce in those trying times between the depression and World War II, but Dad was an inventive kind of fellow when it came to inexpensive entertainment. Food was often on his mind even before his mid-thirties spread. Many an evening, he arrived at the big ornate house to woo Mother with jars of colossal, green olives and bags of exotic fruit like persimmons and pomegranates he purchased at one of the many fruit stands along Main Street. One evening he brought two rather large sweet white Spanish onions, which he trimmed and peeled with Grandma's big kitchen knife and challenged Mom to a race. Never one to ignore a dare, she chomped into the juicy flesh. With misty eyes, she finished her pungent vegetable before Dad, winning the competition and the right to gloat about it for the many years they would spend together.

They married in June of 1942 after seven years of courtship and only after permission was granted by Pepere Roy. Dad came home from his tour of duty to marry but returned to the battle overseas short months later. His left arm and leg were paralyzed by a devastating head injury in that merciless war, requiring Mom to be fairly independent in the early years of their marriage.

When we were on holidays at Petersfield, Mom was the one called upon to fix the things that fell in disrepair or were broken by reckless handling and overuse, things like Memere's lawnmowers. As I remember, she seemed to get most of the odd jobs, things no one else wanted or couldn't do. One week, she spent hours scouring away rust and brushing the insides of the rain barrels with an aluminum-based, silver paint. Most days she emerged, her face red with the heat and her dark brown hair twinkling brightly with little starry splatters of paint.

Rainwater was caught in those barrels from downspouts on each of the house's four corners. The one closest the back door, just outside of the porch, was used to wash dishes because it had the best screen over the top, even so, the water was still alive with wiggling mosquito larvae and ripples of creepy water insects.

An oversized, aluminum kettle kept on the wood stove was used specifically to warm the water for washing body parts most sensitive to the cold. Auntie raved about how soft and clean her hair became when washed in this "gift from the clouds". I just remember when walking around after a good rinse, my hair, filled with electricity, collected errant pieces of lint and waved erratically with the slightest movement.

Mom was always dangling precariously from a ladder somewhere or spent hours disinfecting germ-ridden things like chamber pots or the biffy with alcohol or Lysol from her medicine chest. I hated the backhouse. It always smelled bad and was inhabited by nagging flies and spiders, which I was sure were laying in wait just for me. It was the one place I spent as little time as needed, holding my breath

24

and squatting high over the hole as possible so nothing could jump up and bite me. Mom brought our old toilet seat from home as if it, in some way, would make the suffocating, odorous place seem more comfortable.

Mom never traveled without her big medicine chest and was always making sure that we practiced proper hygiene. "Mrs. Wash-up" was pinned on her because she was always the one who summoned us to wash our hands before meals. She was noted for her strong clear and yes, loud voice, which could be heard breaking the stillness of the creek and surrounding areas. Her voice could even be recognized above the din of Memere's most powerful lawnmower.

As a teenager, on hot lazy afternoons I would often try hiding out somewhere around Chesley's resort, flirting with the tan skinned boys who could usually be found swimming or fishing from the maze of gray floating docks. About 5 p.m., Mom's voice and the sound of Pepere's old dinner gong would resound across the water, lifting flocks of ducks to the air and waking sleeping dogs. People would snicker and grin at each other. I smiled and snickered along with them, then slipped away unnoticed, to wash up for dinner.

Mom has always hidden her shyness under an outgoing exterior fooling most who think they really know her. She enjoys her own company and has passed these traits to my brother and me. She has always been surrounded with people even in her youth, living in the big house on Luxton. As well as being the family haven, the house was home to extended family, a couple of maids and a chauffeur and was usually the setting for festive, clan gatherings. With so many people always at her elbow, the only time she was alone as a child, was when she slept or dressed herself in her warm closet on frigid winter mornings, sometimes falling asleep in its dark coziness. She married Dad from home and then her privacy was completely invaded when she gave birth, as children demand all time and attention till they die- or you do. I know that she must have cherished those moments after Dad had left for work and my brother and I were off to school on breakfasts of toast and tea. Those moments would be short lived as her attention was almost always in demand from visiting neighbors, the constantly ringing telephone and the interruptions of her routine by one of the parish priests who used our corner house to cut through on the way to visit his mother. Father Barker, whom we called "Father Candy", would burst through the back door, pass through the kitchen, maybe picking up a muffin or doughnut and exit through the front door situated in the living room, but not before depositing on the mantle, a few frosted mints or licorice toffees from his bottomless pockets.

Mom introduced herself to many of Petersfield's year-round residents and hired local carpenters and handymen to remodel the staircase to the second floor and install teleposts to insure the main floor did not end up in the basement. As she got to know many people in town, they became accustomed to seeing our faces and were more tolerant of our idiosyncrasies, especially at church.

Mom contributed our share of the foodstuffs to be consumed during our stay. She brought big brown bags and cardboard boxes filled with cookies, fruit, vegetables and a gallon jug of lemon drink concentrate she made from her grandmother's old recipe book. In the early part of the century, the syrup, which was coaxed to a rich yellow hue by a liberal dose of food coloring, was used to treat lumbago. Bright bottles of red, blue, yellow and green food coloring stood in the front row of most well equipped kitchens in those days. It would have been a shame to present cakes of just plain white when a rainbow effect could assault the eye. There was a time when the homemade pickles that graced our table during big family dinners were so green they almost glowed and red and blue devilled eggs were served not only at Easter.

Mom and Auntie also brought to Petersfield, pic-a-pop bottles filled with their own homemade root beer. One of the ingredients had to be purchased from the pharmacist and the elixir erupted when opened, spewing sweet foam over anyone unfortunate to be within spewing distance. Quiet, scorching afternoons would find Mom pulling the blinds down in every room and inviting all of us to jugs of her sweet yet tart lemon drink, served from a perspiring jug, clinking with crowded ice-cubes.

When Mom was not washing the hardwood floors or mending the unmentionables Memere would bring in her suitcase, she was usually hammering the head on an old rake or repairing something that had seen better days.

One evening, Memere was experiencing difficulties starting her one of her most powerful lawn mowers so she called Mom to remedy the problem. With one sandaled foot planted firmly on the machine, Mom pulled the starter cord. The mower sprang to life with a smoky roar, leaping up to remove the tip of the big toe on her right foot. She immediately hobbled into the house, calling for cotton towels and the big brown bottle of hydrogen peroxide from her medicine chest. She poured it over the injured digit, producing a mountain of red foam, which melted into the old hardwood floors. Mr. Chesley, from the resort up the road was called upon to transport Mom to Selkirk Hospital in his station wagon. After their departure, Memere stood in the living room amid the bloodstains and crimson towels. She turned to me and said, "your mother, your mess, clean it up", then left me alone in the room to deal with dreadful happening. At eleven years old I could not imagine what was happening to my mother; it was the kind of event of which nightmares are made. Years passed before I could forgive my grandmother for doing this to me, in fact I wonder if I ever really have. I suppose it is time.

Mom soon returned with stitches, bandages and hospital stories. I recall her saying she felt quite silly lying on a table in the bright, white operating room with only her mutilated toe poking from a small hole in a large green sheet, which covered her entire body. The young doctor was openly flirting with the nurse, mentioning something about skinny-dipping after work, while pushing six stitches into the injured little piggy. Mr. Chesley kindly waited for Mom and took her for a soda in one of the open-air summer stands in Selkirk before bringing her safely back home. Whenever I saw Mr. Chesley after that day, I swear I could detect a halo hovering faintly above his grimy old fishing hat.

We managed to survive our holidays at Petersfield considering few safety precautions were ever taken. Mom was always ready for disaster with her big medicine chest, bursting with bandages, headache powders and gaping wound disinfectants. Very often she would resort to old natural remedies such as applying greasy, cured pork rinds to horse fly bites and once she used the ice cubes from the lemonade she had made that morning.

My little brother, Andre presented himself to her, a stream of cherry red blood oozing from the top of his head. He had accidentally punctured his little noggin with the claw hammer while trying to trap a gopher in the barn. Mom grabbed the ice from the lemonade and held it to the injury. For some unknown reason it worked, shrinking and scabbing or maybe nature just took its course. Anyway, Mom drooped with relief after the fact and we drank warm lemonade that day.

Memere was our resident firebug. She would set flame to the stacks of grass clippings we the peons, would gather all day long. There was always a smudge hanging low over the property in the evenings and at least one smoldering mound with a ribbon of smoke rising every day. Cousin Phil, when about seven or eight, wandered through one of Memere's cinder piles, setting his little running shoes on fire. Auntie's boyfriend, Nick patted his feet to extinguish the flames, but not soon enough. The great medicine chest provided Ozenol ointment, but he would eventually require professional medical attention and long painful treatments

One Sunday evening, Mom, Andre and I were left behind to await the arrival of Dad and his pal Alex on Monday. Uncle Tommy had a full car and the thought of riding all the way to Winnipeg in the back of Nick's truck was unthinkable. A storm was brewing east of us and a big wind was beginning to audibly buffet the sturdy old house. As the darkness grew, Mom noticed orange and yellow flickering in one of the larger scorched stacks near the orchard. With each gust of wind came flames accompanied by many Hail Marys. Andre, being young and fearless thought it a wonderful adventure watching the uncontrolled fire and hearing wild animals seeking refuge in our screenless basement. Despite his pleas, Mom would not allow him to explore the dark lower level. She instead, secured the latch to the basement door and turned to the television for diversion. Andre was very impressed with the usually unavailable "Red Owl Theatre" and American stations on the small black and white set, due to the excess of electrical activity in the skies. He always did and still does, enjoy things that most people find uncomfortable or eerie.

I guess Mom's unshakable faith in God and the years of Hail Marys that permeated the life of that old house worked. After about a half hour of blinding sheet lightening and ground shaking thunder, the kind of which makes one hunch their shoulders and squint, we were hit with a deluge of driving rain which arrived in waves and swamped the low lying areas in the yard, extinguishing the bonfire to black sogginess before it could wreak havoc on the bountiful fruit trees and old barn.

The barn was inhabited by many of nature's creatures, which, if their home had been destroyed, would have also looked to our basement for shelter. The basement was already the retreat for many crawly-looking creations of God, attached to filmy gray threads and hanging from the ceiling beams to brush against my face in the gloom or inhabit and nest in my long thick hair.

Andre was a very curious child, and fearless to say the least. He is six years younger than I, which is not now the considerable gap it was then. Sometimes I would resent Mom's insistence that I watch over him, but at the same time I marveled at his intrepidness and capabilities. He was always striving to be an equal to the rest of us and at times became a real strain on Mom. One time, she finally relented to his constant request to go boating. She compromised by tying a long rope from the dock to the canoe allowing him to spend hours paddling from one end of the property waterfront to the other. Andre found this to be satisfactory at the time and requested the limited excursions most sunny afternoons.

Andre spent many hours poking around in holes and under rocks with his trusty B.B. gun in hand, flushing out gophers and other hapless rodents. His Davy Crockett coon-tailed hat with the leatherette crown and fringed buck-skinned jacket were worn with pride and his imagination carried him to a Petersfield of the past the rest of never knew existed.

Mom was not your run-of-the-mill housewife. She longed for the freedom of spending Saturdays downtown at Eaton's Department Store, jostling for bargains with other escapee homemakers, bowling with the ladies of the CWL on Wednesday afternoons in the basement lanes at Polo Park and teaching the children at St. Ignatius School to become misers by saving their pennies in accounts with the school Credit Union. She has always been a nighthawk and in those days, she did most of the laundry, mending and dusting in the wee hours of the morning. Wrinkles were pressed from Dad's white work shirts while listening to soap operas on the radio as well as the television and she always wrote letters under the small living room lamp, in the quiet, well after everyone else had gone to bed. She loved to dance and despite Dad's inability to accommodate her passion, she foxtrotted with friends and family at weddings and socials and hosted a square-dancing club of eight or ten enthusiastic dosey-doers in our unfinished basement. Mom hung blankets from the rafters to hide the monstrous oil-burning furnace and Dad's workbench cluttered with unfinished projects and sprinkled powdered wax on the flaking maroon painted cement floor most Friday nights during the mid 1950's. My brother and I were lulled to sleep by the low, rich voice of the man calling the moves, the swishing of full, starched crinoline-puffed skirts and the country flavor of songs the likes of" Little Red Wing".

Mom was a master at organizing events; this was something she loved, the bigger, the better, her specialty being fundraisers. She belonged to every organization in the church and school excluding, of course, the altar boys' club and Knights of Columbus. Our supper hours were very often forgotten as she donned white, cotton gloves and sorted through mountains of donated rummage items for spring and fall sales and canvassed the local merchants for Copper Carnival prizes. The Copper Carnival was the highlight of the year, being like a giant silent auction, boasting a hundred prizes. Sheets of one hundred penny tickets were sold for a dollar and those anticipating a bit of luck, deposited the tickets into the box in front of the corresponding prize. They then joined into the other festivities till the draws were made about nine o'clock in the evening. Children were lured to the "Fish Pond", pulling in second-hand presents and the adults to the long table offering strong coffee and sweet, glazed donuts. My brother and I, not being the luckiest carrots in the bunch, would wait at home in anticipation for Mom to return after the church hall clean up, hoping she would come with our winnings in hand. She never let us down, bursting through the door with the wonderful news that we had won a full box of sweet, glazed donuts and we never once, questioned our luck.

In the nineteen-fifties, Mom joined the Stony Mountain Penitentiary chaplain's study club, attending mass behind bars and selling inmates' crafts, raising money to cover rehabilitation costs. One year, Father Bedford's coffers were getting low, so Mom decided she might be able to help the cause. She took advantage of the Catholics' addiction to bingo by offering vouchers to an event in our newly renovated basement.

On the appointed evening, our recreation room was a fog of blue cigarette smoke and bustling with boisterous gamblers. Every seat was filled along lengthy picnic and square card tables lining the walls and occupying the center of the floor. There was even one unexpected couple relegated to play bingo sitting on folding chairs at a table beside the furnace in the unfinished part of the basement. Auntie Emma sold tickets for fifty-cent donations and Dad accepted them in trade for the mixed drinks he served from behind his spanking new bar with the hot pink, arborite countertop and shelves of sparkling glass. He proudly served martinis with olives and brandy and Benedictine as well as Jamaican rum with coke and rye on ice in Mom's fine crystal low-ball glasses and snifters. Father Shaughnessy, the pastor from our church came for the festivities and left with a bottle of whisky he purchased from Mom to compensate the priests left on duty at the rectory. The event was such a successful affair, Mom agreed to an encore the following year.

Unlike Memere, Mom seldom played bingo. Memere was a bingo fan to surpass all proportions. She always caught wind when a big event was imminent, once cajoling Mom into accompanying her to a much-touted "Monster Bingo" at the Winnipeg arena. Mom could never say no to anyone let alone, Memere. The tickets to the much-awaited event led them to convenient, more easily accessible seats on the main floor. Unbeknown to them, beneath the floor lay the ice, which would star in the hockey game later that evening. The frigidity from the ice and the machine keeping it frozen, seeped through the ply-wood and up into their feet, setting a glacial chill in their beings that would later be dispelled only by a steamy, hot bath and a warmed snifter of fine brandy.

You'd have thought this fiasco would have dampened Memere's quest to win the ever-elusive jackpot but her enthusiasm would never be crushed. One terrible stormy night she trusted my then, sixteen year-old brother Andre to chauffeur her down highway #9, just past Petersfield to the Wakefield Community Club for their "Jumbo Fall Bingo". Andre battled through the blinding rain and near hurricane-force winds, in his brand new 1967 blue Beaumont as Mom paced the floors at home, reciting Hail Marys and lighting the blessed candles she kept in the cedar chest for such trying occasions. Memere had full confidence in Andre's driving abilities as well as the protection of her big guardian angel, in whom she so fervently believed. She really could not understand Mom's lack of trust in the powers that were appointed to watch over the adventurous and reprimanded her sternly for the doubt.

By the time cousin Camille took the chauffeuring duties usually carried out by Uncle Tommy, Memere was attending bingo six nights a week. His automobile was familiar with the route to every bingo parlor in town. Sunday was the Sabbath, no bingo, at least not for Memere.

Mom has always counted on her faith to pull her through the tough times so she felt it fitting to also worship God during those good times at Petersfield. She would rouse Andre and me early on Sunday mornings. It was hard to drag myself from the bed but the sleepiness was dispelled the moment I stepped outside into the dewy grass. As I would sit on the old gray dock waiting for the others to ready themselves on those church-going mornings, I felt privileged to witness the mist lifting from the surface of the creek to hang in wispy fingers on the air as I inhaled the sweet smell of a new day. I have always enjoyed the peace and tranquility of being alone, but being at one with nature on a cool Petersfield Sunday morning was about as close to heaven as I could imagine. The loons called invisibly from somewhere in the reeds across the creek and bubbles would rise from the murky water beneath the dock. I'd try to picture what was under there and jump in surprise, as a large fish would leap from the water in the middle of the creek, breaking the morning stillness.

Mom would ride in the back of Nick's delivery van with us kids on the short dusty journey to St. Anne's Church. Upon arrival, she'd tumble out the back doors with the rest of us, straighten her dress and hat and march proudly into church. An elderly, wrinkle-faced aboriginal gentleman, whom we later found out to be a chief, made an impression on Mom. He often arrived about ten minutes before the end of mass, and marched right to the front left pew, which for some reason was always left empty. It was as if everyone knew to leave it open for the eminent chief. Mom voiced her thought that maybe he had a long way to come, always arriving so late and looking a little worn and dusty. She felt quite sorry for him until one morning, while waiting for Nick to fetch us home, Auntie Emma looked at Mom in the way sister communicate. Her eyes were motioning Mom to look across the road to the little colorless old cottage situated opposite the church. Mom glanced over just in time to catch sight the chief crossing the threshold of his home through the torn screen door.

Summers in Petersfield taught me many lessons. I learned, no matter how much disinfectant is used, an outhouse always will smell bad, that Bingo is a survivor and no matter how far I go, I will always hear my mother's voice.

The most important thing I have come to realize is, no matter how prepared you are for anything it may never be enough. So, just love the moment and deal with the pain only when and if it comes.

# LOST ADULTHOOD

Dad was a big man who possessed a wonderful sense of humor. His proper name was Henry, but everyone called him Harry, which was very appropriate. Up to the 1980's, his rather large head was crowned with thick, jet-black hair. A red mustache occupied his upper lip and his dark eyebrows were dense and unruly, bearing over soft hazel eyes. Mom bought him a variety of devises over the years, hoping to curb the growth of hair that took up residence in his nose and ears, but nothing really succeeded.

Dad was the biggest kid on our block, his toys being the envy of the entire neighborhood. As the "king of fun," he was self-appointed to entertain friends and family with his grand collection of practical jokes, magic tricks and games.

We would see little of Dad during our summer weeks at Petersfield. This was the place where my grandmother, Memere and her two daughters, Mom and Auntie Emma, took a break from the everyday humdrum of the city. Dad had only a couple of weeks holidays from work each year and preferred to use them doing something he considered more fun. Dad's idea of a good vacation was hunting and fishing, carrying canoes and supplies through the woods and pooping in the bush. He and his buddy Alec ate brewers yeast for a month before their camping trips and, of course, refrained from bathing while in the woods. Dad claimed the pungent body odor mixed with yeasty perspiration warded off black flies and mosquitoes. I expect it would have also kept cougars and black bears at bay. Dad would arrive home smelling somewhat like a skunky beer, prompting Mom to wash his clothing in chlorine bleach to make them once again inhabitable. While sleeping, the odors emanating from his body permeated the sheets right through to the mattress and remained embedded till at least Christmas despite Mom's efforts involving talcum powders, Lysol spray and liberal morning sprinklings of "Evening in Paris" eau de cologne.

On the subject of perspiration, Dad had a penchant for strong green curry. Whenever Mom made a lovely Irish stew, he'd pour curry over his mountainous plate, indulging himself as the perspiration poured from his forehead. His face always turned a bright red and he would laugh as we'd flee the kitchen, coughing and sputtering on the fumes and not just from the curry.

Alec drove Dad down to Petersfield most Sundays and they always came to pick us up at the end of our holidays. While there, Dad spent hours hiding behind buildings and bushes, his little 8mm movie camera pressed to his right eye, recording everyone's worst profiles. Taking numerous tracks of Mom exiting the little out-house in various states of disarray, he spliced them into other films of unrelated subjects, providing hours of laughter at family dinners and parties for years to come.

Dad loved children and they as well, were drawn to him. Petersfield weekends were no exception. He took us all for rides in the canoe, teaching us how first, to use the paddles and then eventually to operate his little 3 ½ h.p. outboard motor. Organizing baseball games, he appointed himself pitcher because of his inability to run. He even fashioned a miniature golf course on the idle land near the barn and talked Alec into donating his old golf clubs.

Dad related to children better than most of the adults in our family, probably because he lost his adulthood in 1943, in a dusty hot Sicilian town during the war. He was wounded by a sniper, which forced him to endure cranial operations and grueling therapies. He capably brought home the bacon and kept his little family from harm. Beyond that, he was mostly interested in savoring every bit of the fun things this life had to offer. Determined to be a child again, he took all of us with him on his joyous journeys.

Dad prodded Alec into joining him in all kinds of outlandish projects. One winter, they constructed a big wooden boat in our basement. Muted buzzing sounds from the circular saw and drill wafted up through the basement air vents most evenings along with a smattering of thuds and mumblings and everything downstairs was covered in an ever-thickening layer of sawdust. They finally painted the boat white with red trim and in the spring, it was complete and ready to row. Unfortunately, they had to take the craft apart to remove it from the basement. Dismantling the stairs was being considered before Mom caught wind and put an immediate halt to such plans. That was probably a good thing, because the boat was extremely heavy and would have been difficult to get up the stairs in one piece anyway.

Like many things that were considered valuable at one time, Dad's red and white creation was eventually retired to Petersfield.

Our house at Petersfield was like most cabins, a kind of old bones yard. It became the last home for over-used kitchen utensils, linens and the lawn furniture Dad made from the same heavy wood he used for the boat. Whenever Memere sat in one of the chairs, she would slide down into the abyss, calling for help to remove her from the bum-pinching device.

When the old boat arrived at Petersfield, Nick, Auntie's boyfriend, was the most excited. Rowing the boat would flex his muscles and show them off to their full potential. The men and boys carried the bulky craft to the creek bank and slipped it into the water beside the dock. Nick was delighted as he stepped off the dock and onto the middle seat. He sat straight, with a sweet smile on his usually pursed lips as the boat sank like a rock to the muddy bottom. It seemed the old thing had spent two winters and a summer laying idle before coming to Petersfield. It was dry as a bone and took on water like a dehydrated bean. The old soldier was raised the next day, emptied out and lived to ferry us around Netley Creek for a few more years. It eventually began to spring some major leaks making it too dangerous to use, so it was dragged ashore and once more, left to dry out in the hot summer sun.

One evening, Mom noticed we had built a particularly large pile of grass clippings for Memere to burn. She gathered us kids, as well as Auntie Emma and we all dragged the old boat to the big stack. A little gasoline and a match provided us with the biggest bonfire any of us had ever seen. Memere, our resident firebug, was in ecstasy. We roasted wieners and marshmallows, singed the hair on our arms and Mom and Auntie dried wet bathing suits. The firelight was so bright, it reflected on the sparkling creek and lit up the whole yard. Our Netley Creek neighbors must have thought it was morning.

There was an array of colorful critters at Petersfield, most of which I never saw in the city. There were a lot of gophers, pelicans and red-winged black birds, to name a few. Auntie would leave the fish guts on the creek bank for nightly skunk visits, insuring she didn't have stinky garbage and the little black and white visitors had fishy morsels to eat. One beautiful breezy day, while I was

39

raking and Memere was cutting grass behind the orchard, she thought she spied cousin Phil hiding among the bushes and trees in his usual quest to avoid raking the ever mounting grass clippings. Auntie Emma joined Memere in booming out orders for Phil to show himself. Within seconds, the green foliage rustled violently and out stepped three of the biggest wild turkeys I have ever seen. Actually, before that moment, I had never seen one. Memere and Auntie turned and ran for the protection of the porch, screaming all the way. The expended energy was really unnecessary because the large feathered beasts simply melted back into the denseness of the orchard. After supper that evening, Mom went down the gravel road to Chesley's resort to use the phone. She called Dad and requested he bring his rifle with him on Sunday. There was something of substantial size residing in the barn that might pose a threat to us kids. I'm sure she was also thinking of succulent, brown turkey drumsticks with cranberry sauce.

The "great white hunter" arrived as appointed on Sunday; rifle in hand to perform the requested task. Dad looked like the Pied Piper, surrounded by a gaggle of kids, moving toward the big dark barn and whatever lurked within. Shots rang out and we all gasped as furry and not so furry things scurried, fleeing the old barn. Our frightening creature turned out to be a mangy old groundhog, whose lead-riddled carcass was paraded around by the boys. Linda, Yvonne and I felt a bit squeamish about the whole thing but Phil and Andre spent a good half hour holding the dead animal at shoulder height, while posing with puffed chests in front of my old Brownie camera. There were no great trophies or turkey dinners that day, but all was not lost. Dad brought a set of paper targets, which he tacked to one side of the barn. He taught a hunter safety course and marksmanship to air cadets on Friday nights, so he was well trained to give us all a short lesson and each a couple of turns to try and hit the targets.

Dad always had something up his sleeve besides his arm. One Sunday, just as the final licks of green paint were being applied to the new out-house, he decided it would be a good idea to have a formal initiation. Toilet paper was tied around the little two seated structure and Uncle Tommy cut the" ribbon" before welcoming Nick, the first to officially make use of the spanking new facility. Memere pinned a red rose on his plaid shirt when he emerged red faced, as Dad's little movie camera hummed away, freezing the event for future entertainment.

Dad passed away in August of 1991 after suffering a series of strokes. His doctor said it could have been the consequences of years of smoking and ingesting all those decadent pastries and legions of burgers and fries. To Dad, those cream puffs and jelly donuts were a bonus. He should have been dead forty-eight years before, under siege, down that dusty little street in Sicily. As it was, his left leg and arm were completely paralyzed. He seldom told anyone and few noticed. He couldn't run or drive a car, but he could fool everyone into believing he could.

I learned many things those Sundays at Petersfield with Dad. I learned new outhouses only smell new for one day, yeast is not only used for making bread, and wild turkeys can make old people run fast.

Most importantly, I learned that the human spirit can overcome any adversity when woven tightly with the laughter and naivety of a child.

# FISH TALES

Fifteen and sixteen year-old boys are a curious lot. I would often gaze at my son while in his mid teens and wonder what secrets he held deep within himself. Most boys start off life open-faced and honest but as the years stretch into double digits, many become secretive and sneaky. I have observed this tradition for many years, not only with my son but also with my brother, cousins and friends.

Petersfield summers passed and our little city boys changed with the eroding creek banks and moldering old barn. As things broke down, they grew up, building their personalities one experience at a time. In 1958 my brother Andre was eight years old, still young and cute enough to get away with just about anything. He was like a little sponge, soaking up all the big boys had to offer, both good and bad.

Despite the six-year gap in our ages, Andre and I are very close. Just thinking of him gives me a feeling of fullness where I know my soul must be. There is a mute understanding of support we hold for each other that will only be dissipated with death. This promise of demise was uttered many times in our youth also because of the wide difference in our ages. I was routinely expected to entertain and chaperone this unruly, restless minded little fellow who wasn't ever in the least bit interested in my company or I in his.

Little Andre's unharnessed imagination carried him through cloudless blue skies in a steak of light and under Netley Creek, swimming with the schools of perch or lazing in the mud bottom with gurgling crayfish. His fertile mind was his best friend in Petersfield because he was the youngest; no one was near his age. I would take him to Chesley's to buy bags of candy and he spent time on the dock fishing with Victor, but he seemed to prefer his own company. He was always the first to bed when the rest of us were playing cards and he was the first to rise in the morning when we were all lazily sleeping late.

Andre was seldom idle and usually quiet. It is said when a child is quiet he is often up to no good but with Andre, it was hard to tell. For him, everything he did became a learning experience, something he would carry through life, trapped in chambers somewhere in that little head of his. His insatiable curiosity directed him to dismantle all his mechanical toys within hours of receipt. He eventually graduated to electrical appliances, ripping gusts from radios and televisions, leaving the shells for us to deal with. To this day, Mother's basement is littered with the carcasses from Andre's past and every television in my house is perfectly tuned.

Andre was young enough that he spent a lot of time with the adults when we vacationed at Petersfield. This was no picnic for him, I'm sure. He was a light eater, food not being the center of his universe like it was for the rest of us. We ate from the moment we opened our eyes in the mornings, snacking on the chips and chocolates we had earned from the day before. There were always bowls of green grapes on the kitchen table and cool red watermelon in the refrigerator along with jugs of sweet, ice-cold lemonade and homemade root beer. Auntie and Memere were unduly concerned about Andre's lack of appetite and determined something was wrong with him. They endeavored to scare him into eating, claiming he would cease to grow and telling him, in fact he would probably become smaller. They called him "Tiny Tim"; laughingly saying he would be lost in the grass to be run over by Memere's lawn mower. With his colorful imagination, this must have been a terrifying thought, the fodder of which nightmares are made. Mom tried to soothe his mind but found it difficult to oppose the opinions of her mother and older sister who shadowed her in their largeness of presence.

Mom had an immense aversion to flies. The house was filled with spools of sticky, mustard colored paper, dangling from the ceilings and glistening with bug bodies, some dead, some still wiggling. She had a big collection of multi-colored fly swatters, one for each person in the house and extras for visitors. There would be a fly killing session at least twice throughout the day and usually before meals. If any of those nasty winged insects dared to set one hairy foot on the food Mom set out for Andre and me, the plate would be immediately emptied into the deep blue trash bin under the sink. Mom always reasoned out loud that one never knew where the flies had been. Auntie Emma's kids got to eat everything; she wasn't really bothered. To this day, I cannot knowingly consume anything a fly had sat upon and I have considerately passed this squeamishness on to my son.

Cool, rainy days at Petersfield were never as boring as in the city. I suppose it was because we cousins were all together and that was fun in itself. We entertained each other by playing card games, listening to music and telling stories. Fishing was something we all had in common. Even on those rainy days, Victor could be counted on to have a line or two dangling from the dock, his rod anchored with rocks from the shore. Not a moment went by when one of our red and white line floats wasn't bobbing over the weeds on Netley Creek.

The dock could become a hot place in the sizzling days of summer. It was also uncomfortable with splintering wood and no place to lean your back. Victor figured out how to make himself really comfortable. He pulled out an old wicker chair from the living room and padded it with a couple of comfy old cushions and positioned it in the middle of the dock. Most sunny days, he'd plop a straw hat on his curly head and cast a line way out past the lily pads. Sometimes when the water was high, he had more luck just dropping the line off the end of the dock. Victor had a pensive soul, which manifested itself in his demeanor. His face held the seriousness of an adult from the time he was five years old, with piercing eyes under a fixed, furrowed brow and a mouth that could cut you in two with few words. Even before reaching the ripened age of sixteen, Victor was the man of Auntie's house; handily wielding his authority over whomever he felt did not behave in an appropriate manner. Nick very often took the brunt of his wrath, awaking some mornings from nights of too many rye cocktails with his eyes bleary, his face stuck to the oil-clothed kitchen table and wincing painfully from the siren in his ears that was Victor's voice.

Victor spent hours by himself on the old gray dock, staring into the ripples on the water. He took extreme pleasure in pulling a rare species from the opaque, green water near the shore. Anything that wasn't a whiskered bullhead or green striped perch was, to us, considered rare. Jackfish were not regular visitors under our dock, but once in a while a young one would come nosing around. One time we were privy to catching a glimpse of this magnificent toothy fish when young Andre was landing his catch. The hook presented him with a small perch upon which was attached a good-sized jack. He was only about eight years old at the time and the sight froze him in awe, still holding the duo above the water. I was glued to my seat and gazed agog long enough that the jack fish relinquished it's dinner and fell back into the green water with a splash. Poor Andre stood there for a moment, staring at his scarred perch then turned to me with a pained expression of disappointment on his little, freckled face.

Andre never took defeat lying down, not even when little. He turned the episode into his own elaborate fish story, which he recanted to everyone who looked remotely interested. He couldn't wait till Dad arrived on the weekend, because Dad always found everything we did to be a great adventure.

There were certain early morning rituals strictly adhered to when vacationing in Petersfield. The most reliable ones were the making of aromatic coffee set in the bubbling pot on the big, black and silver wood stove and Auntie Emma's first cigarette of the day. When teenagers, Victor and Philip would set out every morning about seven, the boat packed with sandwiches, potato chips and jugs of iced lemonade for an optimistic morning of fishing. There was usually a friend or two tagging along to try his hand at luring a few catfish into the boat. I think it was a guy thing, part of coming of age, because we girls were never invited along. We asked on occasion and hinted often enough but our answer was usually a mocking chuckle or an abhorrent stare.

There was a particularly nice day, nearing the end of the summer holidays when Glen and Andy accompanied Vic and Phil on their morning observance. Seeing there were four to paddle, they decided to take the canoe. The boat was secured with food staples for the morning, fishing rods and bait, and Glen asked if he could borrow someone's wristwatch so they would know when to be back in time for his ride to the city. No one had a wristwatch so Mom offered my little travel alarm clock. It was ivory colored with gold trim, the one Dad bought from a little Main Street pawn shop for my thirteenth birthday. They departed with little fanfare as usual, taking the anchor from the motorboat, as the canoe didn't have one. In actuality, we didn't have an anchor for the motorboat either. We used a white cinder block tied with a length of heavy rope and this is what they took with them. After about twenty-five minutes, they found just the right spot in the marsh; the place one of them would finally pull up the "big one".

It was a perfect day, not too hot, not too cold, the sky, a quilt of blue and white, dotted with paunchy pelicans, scanning the waters for breakfast. Philip secured the rope to one of the seats in the canoe and threw the cinder block over the side, into the reflecting, green water. This particular day, the water was too high or the rope was too short. Before the anchor reached the muddy bottom, it suddenly pulled taut, flipping the canoe and unceremoniously dumping its contents into the marshy water and reeds. Philip, Glen and Andy popped to the surface along with the bags of sandwiches and lemonade jug. Not finding Victor, who couldn't swim, the boys took turns submerging, all the while frantically feeling through the thick, murky water. In their frustration, they decided to flip over the canoe, climb in and think rationally about what to do next. Philip was already rehearsing in his mind what he was going to tell Auntie and Yvonne. Glen ducked under the water and came up under the canoe in an effort to turn it upright from beneath. In doing so, he came face to face with a terrified Victor.

When the craft flipped over, Victor was hanging on

to both sides with all his might, ending up in the merciful air bubble between the canoe and the water. Hearing the other panicked voices, he could say nothing as he was frozen with fear. All was well in an instant as the trio scrambled into the canoe, pulling a well-shaken Victor in behind them. They sat and stared at each other as if in a trance, holding their breaths then melted into laughter and relief. They no longer had the heart to fish, not that they could what with all their equipment permanently residing in the soft, marsh floor. The sandwiches were floating down the rippling channel along with hopes of catching something other than a chill, as they were all soaked and smelling like the fish they went there to bag.

Paddling back to our welcoming dock took about ten minutes faster than it took to go out. I guess they were impatient to recant their harrowing experience. They relished in the horrified looks on our faces and retold the episode to our willing ears, enhancing the details more each time. Soon the excitement wore off as the story grew old and I just felt heavy-hearted about my little lost clock.

I learned many things during those summers at Petersfield. I learned that one never knows where flies have been, not to use cinder blocks as anchors and fishing is a good thing.

Most importantly, I learned that you should try to recapture the imagination you had as a child. It can still carry you to wonderful places far beyond your physical reach and some too wonderful to even exist in this world.

Little Andre afloat in Dad's big boat

# FISH GUTS AND RED NAIL POLISH

$A$untie Emma's presence stands out in my mind when I think of those summer weeks she and her children joined Mom, my brother Andre and me at Petersfield to breathe in the sweet country air. Memere would also be there to oversee our activities during those wonderful vacations.

Auntie Emma was, in reality, my grandmother's fourth child. Memere's first son Buster died of diphtheria at age two and her second son was stillborn. Uncle Tommy subsequently became her oldest, Mom her youngest and Auntie Emma was sandwiched in between, the middle child.

Auntie was assaulted by polio at a very young age. She endured grueling therapies and the application of braces on the affected leg. Time was spent under hot foments and the hands of hopeful massagers and hours trickled away while sitting on hard chairs in the beige waiting rooms of doctors promising cures. Despite the remedies, she would be imparted with a stunted leg and foot that was a source of pain and annoyance throughout her life.

Auntie lived in the big white house with green trim, on Luxton avenue which was the original family home of my great grandparents. The house boasted a large country style kitchen, formal dining room with a table and chairs enough to seat at least twenty-five to thirty, a cozy bay windowed living room and adjoining sitting room in a corner of which sat an old out-of-tune upright piano. There were two staircases to the second floor, one was enclosed, rising from the kitchen and the other presented an ornately carved handrail directing the way from the large front foyer up to the six bedrooms branching from three hallways. A small, widow's walk jutted to the outside from behind two doors on the second floor but was seldom used. Auntie remained in the house after her husband Victor's sudden death, trying her hand at many occupations in an effort to support her three children, Victor, Philip and Yvonne. She eventually settled on a career selling Avon products, building a cosmetics sales empire from her home. The dining room buffet was always well stocked with a variety of perfumes, creams and skin cleansers. Even on the day she died there was still an artistic display of lipsticks, nail polish and beauty products on her buffet.

Auntie Emma was an attractive dark-haired brown-eyed lady, what men used to call, "a handsome figure of a woman." Despite the concerns of the matrons in the family that Auntie's infirmity would serve to prove her unworthy of men's attentions, many a gent was drawn strongly to her beauty and reckless, fun-loving ways.

Auntie's appearance was very important to her, as it was imperative to look her best considering the business she was in. The cosmetic case she brought on our Petersfield holidays was almost as large as Mom's medicine chest and to her, I'm sure it was just as essential. Whenever unexpected guests surprised us, she disappeared into her bedroom and later would emerge with earrings, red lipstick and rouge and long trousers.

Auntie was our chief cook and pie maker. She prepared our freshly caught fish, no matter how small or ugly. The only stipulation was on the condition someone else killed them, which was no problem; we just gave them to cousin Philip first. He was a grubby little kid who was always poking his nose into all the dark and dirty places on the property. His pockets were usually stuffed with wiggly pink worms, assorted frogs legs and things I'd rather not think about. On occasion he missed a fish or maybe it was just playing possum. Poor Auntie would scream when it suddenly came alive, flipping and flopping on her kitchen counter. Fish guts dangled from the countertops and scales flew, but through it all, her hands always showcased immaculate, long red fingernails.

Femininity came natural to her and it did not go unnoticed by the opposite sex. She had her share of suitors but Nick was the object of her affections when we were youngsters on holidays at Petersfield. He spent every weekend and the odd weekday with us.

Nick was a former wrestler, a combination of muscle bound and obese with rosebud lips, a large, square head and two hammer-toes he would wiggle to make us kids laugh. A butcher by trade, he provided most of the meat for our country table. We dined on different exotic delicacies, pork hocks, beef kidneys and Auntie once presented a steaming platter of roasted pigtails. My brother Andre was constantly being harassed for his finicky appetite. Was it any wonder?

Nick was fond of his whisky. Most nights, he and Auntie would lounge on the porch with Memere and Mom after the sunset and the breeze died. The heavy, warm air carried their voices to the darkness of my bedroom. I could hear the clinking of ice-cubes and stifled giggles from the depth of my musty pillows. No matter how much perfumed talc Mom sprinkled in the beds, they still held that damp winter odor.

One moonless night, out of curiosity, I left my bed to find the source of uncontrollable laughter ringing through the barely lit house. It seemed Nick had washed down one too many drinks and decided to relieve himself outside in the inky darkness. Miscalculating the distance to the creek, he dropped into the cool water with a huge splash and fortunately sobered up enough to save himself. He stumbled back to the house, soaking wet, covered with snails and weeds and his shoes were full of slimy gray muck.

There were other times when he'd become drunk and we'd beg him to perform skits for us. He'd comb his dark hair low to one side of his forehead and fashion a square mustache out of a band-aid and black shoe polish. He then strutted around the living room, right arm outstretched, spewing pig-German and reducing us to tears of laughter. Other times he danced something he called the Kolomeyka, squatting low, arms crossed on his chest and kicking one bent leg in front of the other. The boards in the floor buckled as dust flew and we thought surely he would break through the old hardwood and fall to the basement.

Auntie loved her garden, laying claim to a sizeable section of land right beside the shady orchard and in front of the old gray barn. Mom was never in contention over garden space as she hated gardening and left the planting and weeding to those more interested. Auntie Emma had a vegetable patch in the city but it paled in comparison to the plot she tended at Petersfield. Hours passed as she planted onions, carrots and plenty of lettuce for sour cream salads and there was a rhubarb clump so large; it would go to seed before everyone could harvest the fruit. Mom would often pull a few stalks, wash and serve them with small bowls of dipping sugar.

Auntie could be found weeding her garden any time of the day or evening. It was probably therapeutic for her. She never minded getting earth under those beautiful red fingernails, not that they stayed dirty for long. I expect she must have tired sometimes of looking the picture of gentility and just needed to play in the mud.

Auntie possessed the kind of temper that sent small animals scurrying. It certainly kept her boys in line. Philip especially, was in trouble more often than not. I was thankful to be Mom's kid rather than Auntie's, when she was angry. One time I voiced my childish opinions and she didn't say much, she didn't have to; that look of hers was enough.

I'm sure Auntie was a daring girl because her eyes always had that knowing glint and she always seemed to have an inkling when we were up to no good. When we did something naughty, she was usually just around the corner, soon to catch us in the act.

Twice a week, Auntie would lug out her cosmetic case and hoist it onto the kitchen table, opening it to reveal many colored and aromatic bottles and jars. She would treat herself and Memere to an elaborate facial. The two of them would lounge in the living room, white faced and nibbling on cucumber sandwiches and hot sweet tea. Memere always claimed drinking something hot on a warm day served to cool you off. She also swore, her woolen undershirt kept her cool in the hot afternoon sun. I never believed her.

When I was about ten or eleven, I thought the application of all Auntie's goop was disgusting, but as puberty crept up on me, I found myself surprisingly interested in Auntie's big cosmetic case. She seemed to enjoy my attention and would give me little samples of pink lipstick and soft, floral perfumes, just what I needed for Sunday church services.

When I became a teenager, I actually enjoyed going to little St. Anne's church early on misty Sunday mornings. One of the influential gentleman farmers in the area would enter the church and march down the carpeted middle aisle to the right front pew, wife in tow, followed by one daughter and seven robust, tanned sons. Even on the most humid mornings, he appeared cool and dapper in his three-piece suit and fancy tie, knotted tightly under his chin. He always scratched his ear with a ten-dollar bill before depositing it in the collection plate. I imagine this gesture was to fortify his prominence in the parish. There was one acne-cheeked blond son of the farmer who set a flutter in my young heart. He was about sixteen years old and, sadly for me, not interested in a chubby thirteen year old citified girl.

One Sunday morning, Alec, my Dad's friend, drove him to Petersfield to pick us up. Uncle Tommy usually drove us down and Dad and Alec came to fetch us home at the end of our holiday. Dad brought along his 3 ½ h.p. motor to propel one of the old boats housed in the barn. He chose the big green cargo canoe and invited Auntie and Nick for a scenic tour through the long narrow channel to the mouth of Lake Winnipeg. Auntie looked so pretty as they pulled away from the dock. Dad made sure she was posed in the bow seat so she could see the unobstructed beauty of the channel and lake. Nick was in the middle on the floor, to even the load and Dad played captain, steering the motor. We waved them away and expected their return in about an hour.

Time passed quickly at Petersfield, except of course, if we were toiling under Memere's iron hand. About an hour and a half slipped away before we heard the buzzing of Dad's little motor rounding the bend from the reedy channel onto the glassy green creek. Auntie Emma was still perched in the front of the canoe, only now, she was soaking wet. As they neared the dock, I could see her tightly permed hair resembled sheep's wool with drops of water dangling from each little curl, her mascara streaked black on her cheeks and there was that look in her eyes. Nick was very serious. I'm sure he knew what the consequences of snickering would be. Dad, on the other hand, was grinning widely, his gold inlays glistening in the afternoon sun. Nothing scared Dad. He'd been to war.

He had deliberately placed Auntie in front, knowing the canoe was no match for the waves on the mighty lake. He mercifully only subjected her to five or six sizeable whitecaps before turning back into the serenity of the channel. Dad was always playing nasty jokes at her expense and for some reason, she always let him get away with it.

That Sunday, with grace, and nary a word, she stepped from the canoe onto the dock and across the front lawn to the house. She re-appeared forty-five minutes later, in her kitchen, her hair pulled back under a small scarf. She was sipping on a rye and water and smoking a long slim cigarette held in a silver holder. That evening, she served a large roast of pork dinner with relishes and potato salad. The incident was only mentioned in whispers till many years later when she too would laugh and reminisce about our adventures in Petersfield.

I learned some important things that summer in Petersfield. I learned never to pee outside on a moonless night, never sit in the front of a canoe, and no amount of makeup can withstand the wrath of Lake Winnipeg.

Most importantly, I learned that you will always look good to the ones who love you and almost anything done in honest jest is forgivable.

# UNCLE TOTO

U ncle Tommy, who was affectionately called Uncle Toto, was Memere's oldest child and sole surviving son. We kids called him Uncle Toto because he was the only person in the family who owned a car, which in French is l'auto. Children have a way of innocently tagging others with nicknames, which manage to stick through their entire lives, and so it was with Uncle Toto.

The care and management of the family owned Roblin hotel was a twenty-four hour commitment and Memere would trust no one but Uncle Tommy to oversee the task. Uncle Tommy knew no other kind of work as he was inducted into the hotel business at a very young age, working alongside his mother and taking over the Roblin Hotel at age twenty-one. The hotel would be his home, the place where he brought his bride, raised his children and continued to work, partnered with Memere until the day she died. He then carried on, with his son Camille.

Uncle Tommy came to Petersfield every Sunday, sometimes accompanied by his family or Mom, Andre, Memere, and me, and other times he arrived with a hired man or two from the hotel.

He was married to Auntie Lil, a small, very energetic woman. Although Auntie Lil wasn't in Petersfield the same weeks as we, her garden was, proving Auntie Emma wasn't the only one in the family with "green fingers". Auntie Lil's plot was situated on the southwest corner, unobstructed in the pure sunshine between the orchard and the creek. The earth was brown and rich from silt left there by periodic spring flooding, encouraging the land to transform into a dense vegetable jungle every summer. It was a grand muddle of waving green cucumber leaves, neat rows of lacy carrot tops and a tall patch of golden-tufted corn stalks. We often lost sight of Auntie Lil, as her compact body ventured into the green undergrowth to pick her treasured morsels on the rare weekends we all spent together.

Auntie Lil held a position in nursing before marrying Uncle Tommy and eventually presented him with three children, Bobby, Camille and Cecile. Bob was one month older than I, the others younger.

Auntie Lil shared one of the big bedrooms on the main floor with Mom so we weren't able to take our Petersfield vacations at the same time. She would spend her allotted weeks with her children and sometimes her sister or brother joined them. Auntie was active in the business and school communities and especially the church. One Petersfield, summer vacation saw the back yard dotted with tents inhabited by girl guides from Sacred Heart School. They slumbered the nights away peacefully, under the moonlit diamond studded sky, tucked in the sleeping bags Auntie managed to finagle for a good cash price from the man at the wholesale. It was such a good deal, she bought each one of us kids a cozy colorful sleeping bag for Christmas that year.

Auntie Lil added a softer side, a feminine touch to the lives of the lodgers who made the hotel their home. She listened to their problems, cared for their ills and bled for the indignities heaped upon them by society. On Sundays most restaurants were closed, so when she returned from morning Mass she immediately set about cooking breakfast for the hungry old gents. As years wore on it became a family thing, Auntie and her kids breaking dozens of eggs and grilling pounds of bacon. The succulent aromas wafting from the little manager's suite on the second floor would dance lightly down the dimly lit hallways signaling those with empty innards and hungry spirits.

The gentleness that was Auntie Lil would become only memories far too soon for me. She suffered the ravages of lung cancer in her fifties, possibly from the clouds of smoke that rose from the beer parlor day after day. The dreadful disease claimed her mercilessly, leaving the rest of us feeling betrayed by our faith in miracles.

It was appropriate that we gave Uncle Toto his nickname because he had a name for each of us kids. He would tease us unashamedly and changed our nicknames over the years as we accomplished things, bought our cars and became employed. Mom told me he teased her constantly when they were young, embarrassing her when he found out she had done something silly or when her fellas came to call. He named Camille General Croute, a French slang for a crusty turd, because it was his job to clean the backhouse. He called me Air Canada and Phil became Barracuda when he purchased his first car.

Uncle Tommy's old cars were never traded in; they were handed down. Victor, being the oldest of all us children, obtained his drivers license first and inherited Uncle's old maroon Kaiser Fraser with the expansive windshield, huge ivory colored steering wheel and white-walled tires. He was nicknamed Al Capone and resembled something from the "Untouchables", just barely peeking through the steering wheel when cruising around town with the his acne-cheeked, brush-cut buddies in the plump bulky vehicle.

Automobiles were scarce in our neighborhood during

the 1950's and early 60's. Most people living on our block rode the electric trolley buses or walked. Dad couldn't drive and Mom never had the inclination to learn, not that they could have afforded a car anyway. When our presence was required in places inaccessible by foot, bus or taxi, we relied on Dad's best friend Alec and Uncle Tommy.

Alec was almost always available to take us to the hard-to-get-to places and often treated us to Sunday drives. Being friends from their childhoods in the West End of Winnipeg, Dad and Alec had a kind of kinship found in people who have been pals through most of life's stages. They played stickball in the street as children and went hunting and fishing together when forced into adulthood. Dad stood up for Alec in the school grounds and Alec stood up for Dad when he married Mom. Alec was appointed to be my brother's godfather and took the privilege very seriously.

Alec welcomed a wounded Dad home from the war and never once discouraged him from trying to bring to fruition any of his outlandish projects and schemes. He never told Dad there were things a paralytic couldn't do. Simply lending his support, Alec stood by until Dad succeeded or failed; the latter seldom happened, making Alec's job easy.

The two men were like dirt and water, so completely different yet easily blended but not easily separated.

Alec was a bachelor, a rather small man, maybe five-foot three with thinning hair. Wire-rimmed glasses sat pertly on the bridge of his nose and like Dad, he possessed a colorful collection of golf shirts. He was always chewing on an old, aromatic pipe and wore billowing brown trousers. Wide pants were the style of the day but Alec, being so slight, looked like a boat in full sail whenever there was any kind of a breeze. His head was usually topped with seasonal Fedoras, straw in summer, felt in fall and spring and fuzzy borg in winter.

Alec was a bit reclusive, only spending time with his few close friends and immediate family. He had three sisters, Joe being the only one to have children. His sister, Olive was married to a big furry man of substance and then there was Mae, who lived with Alec for a couple of years. Mom would say Mae's thinking was a little slow but she managed to hold down a job at the local Good Will shop. During her idle times, she occupied herself with the domestic duties necessary to keep their little one-bedroom apartment on Balmoral Street tidy and clean. Mae was given the bedroom, while Alec slept on the Toronto couch in the sparsely furnished living room. When I was about nine or ten, Dad would take me on the bus to visit the odd little duo. Mae always served liverwurst sandwiches at the kitchen table and I was always sat on the chair backing to the wall where Alec kept his girlie calendar. Then Dad and Alec played cribbage the rest of the afternoon, letting me move the pegs for them. Mae wasn't much of a cook, so when Alec complimented her on a particularly nice dish, he could count on being served the same thing for many evenings to come. One Saturday afternoon, Alec decided to treat Mae to a movie. He had never done this before, so Mae was very excited. She carefully studied the entertainment section of the paper and made her choice. Thinking they were going to see an animated cartoon, Alec emerged from the theatre only minutes later, red-faced at presenting his very confused sister with a rather risqué movie. Alec never took Mae to another picture show, not that she ever asked.

Most Petersfield holidays ended with Alec driving Dad to pick up Andre, Mom and me. Alec never mingled much with the other adults. While Dad was busying himself entertaining the kids or gabbing with Memere and the gang, Alec would find himself a nice shady tree to stretch out under. Pulling his straw Fedora over his face to ward off the hungry horseflies Alec would snooze the best part of the afternoon away.

Memere and Auntie occasionally mentioned how odd they thought Alec was but never when Dad was within earshot.

Little Alec just seemed to have a problem dealing with a lot of people at one time. He enjoyed the company of a select few and most of the time, just one; himself. Surprising to some, my Dad was also a loner. He loved people, but as well, cherished his solitary moments, claiming he didn't mind his own company and sometimes it was preferred.

Alec and Dad embarked on treks that would take them through the serenity of the Whiteshell Provincial Park every summer until they co-purchased the ¼ section of wild, uncultivated land near Lundar. Their earlier vacations in the Whiteshell were spent portaging through the bush with the long, green aluminum cargo canoe from Petersfield. They would pick it up and bring it home a couple of weeks prior to the trip. Just getting the canoe to stay atop Alec's little gray Austin was a feat in itself, involving ropes, suction cups and guy wires. On the morning of their departure, Mom, Andre and I would stand at the curb to wave as the duo set off, looking somewhat like an ambitious ant trying to manouver a large green leaf. Our neighbors would take a moment from their Saturday chores to marvel at the spectacle moving down their front street, slowly picking up momentum. We all thought surely, they would become airborne as they approached highway speed. Dad and Alec spent at least two weeks away at a time, fishing in the clear sparkling waters and paddling the heavy canoe silently past startlingly beautiful displays of nature. I doubt if they ever said much to each other, they were the kind of friends who didn't have to. One look, the shrug of a shoulder or a smile said it all. My brother and I are fortunate enough to have cultivated such friendships ourselves.

One blustery winter day Alec was huddled within his hat and wooly scarf. He held his head down against the wind in determination to press his way to the Pancake House for his usual lunch of bacon and eggs, sunny side up. As he was crossing Pembina Highway, he was struck by a car, causing a head injury that would plunge him into a coma which did not lift for two weeks. His body eventually healed to what it was before the accident, but his mind was regretfully altered. He became even more reclusive, spending day after day in his room at the retirement home, seldom answering his phone. I called every week, but received no answer. Seems the only times he ever lifted the receiver was when I rang to tell him of Dad's debilitating stroke and again to inform him of Dad's passing. It was as if he felt the urgency and importance of answering his phone on those two occasions.

Alec died a few years later, in his sleep, fittingly alone in his little room at the retirement home on Pointe Road. The funeral service was private, just what he would have wanted.

Uncle Tommy, on the other hand, was seldom alone; only when sleeping was his mind devoid of the crowded life he lived. But then, there were always his dreams. Who knows?

Uncle Tommy was under the impression that children should earn their keep and holiday time at Petersfield did not relieve us of this serious obligation. Some of the projects he decided appropriate were labor intensive and gathered moans and groans from us every day. Memere was our self-appointed taskmaster, tallying our worth in hours or piecework. One year Uncle Tommy noticed the banks along the creek in front of our place were eroding. It seemed to him a shame to watch valuable property wash away with the lapping waves or occasional high water. He decided a load of rocks from the quarry not far from

63

Clandeboye would do just the trick. He arranged to have a big load of multi-colored rocks and stones dumped in a pile just beside the house, about a hundred feet from the creek. We were each issued a galvanized pail and payment of one stale chocolate for every third trip we made from the pile to the shore. The mountain of rocks seemed so immense to us as we picked away at it day after day, not creating any noticeable difference. It took us an eternity, in our children's minds, to move the blight from the lawn to the edge of the water. I must say it was a job well done, although I cannot, to this day, understand why the delivery men didn't just dump the stones along the bank in the first place or at least a little closer to the creek.

I don't recall ever seeing Uncle Tommy clad in anything other than a white, long sleeved shirt, dark trousers and long narrow black lace-up shoes. It was as if he was always ready to go to work. He'd arrive in his big car, survey the property, have something to eat and then snooze in one of the over-stuffed chairs in the living room. We never saw him in fun clothes, blue jeans or a plaid shirt. In fact, I don't really recall ever seeing him have fun. When everyone was out in the yard playing Sunday games of baseball and golf, he was usually deep down in one of the big old chairs or the chesterfield, sleeping off a week's work. Dad sometimes talked him into the boat for a short jaunt on the creek. Dad couldn't stand to see anyone missing out on a good time. He oftentimes traveled Europe solo and urged Uncle Toto to join him on occasion, but to no avail. Uncle showed interest, although Dad knew their wonderful plans would never materialize. He never stopped asking, maybe just to make Uncle Tommy feel that the option was always open.

One breathlessly dark night we were roused by a clamor in the basement. The door to the lower level was always latched, so Mom and Auntie Emma assured us we were in no immanent danger. Uncle Tommy was summoned the next morning to come to Petersfield before he opened the bar. He arrived with an air of self-importance, seemingly proud of the fact that his masculinity was being called upon by his younger sisters and Mother. Clutching Philip's baseball bat in his right hand, he unlatched the basement door and proceeded cautiously down the staircase, which was barely lit by a single low-wattage bulb hanging from a length of wire. He swatted each step with the bat as he descended, the noise echoing off the damp cement walls. Then, the banging abruptly stopped, immediately being followed by a flurry of rising footsteps. Uncle Toto flew through the door, slamming it shut and locking it in one fell swoop. Red-faced and gasping for air, he informed Mom that our basement was now home to a furry little skunk and that maybe she should phone someone local to take care of the problem. Auntie Emma served him a hearty bowl of vegetable soup, a roast beef sandwich and with that, Uncle Toto was out the gate and back on the road to Winnipeg to open up the bar.

A Mr. Scofield was keeping a flock of sheep on Mrs. Veitch's place, the property just west of ours. Mom espied him in the yard that same day while he was tending to business, so she wandered over and asked if he knew anyone who could safely remove a skunk from our basement. Volunteering his own services, he said it was necessary for him to first drop by his home for the proper equipment. He arrived about an hour later with a cage and within five minutes, the little black and white intruder was captured without incident. Mr. Scofield disposed of it in the creek. We never realized back then how precious every wild creature is to the balance of life. Death sentences were imposed on so many animals merely because they got in our way or were so cute, we had to handle them to death. This was true also of the adorable baby bunnies we found in Auntie's tall corn patch and the green, golden-eyed, leopard frogs gathered from the grasses growing along the creek bank. We kids kept the frogs in four-quart glass sealers which Mom and Auntie Emma had the compassion to dump over and set free while we were sleeping. Our dreams of repopulating the city with frogs evaporated that night. Mom feigned ignorance when we asked what possibly could have happened, leaving it to our imaginations. We never once suspected her or Auntie.

One lazy warm afternoon Memere was, as usual, mowing grass, creating her noise and noxious exhaust fumes. Auntie was weeding the garden when she called us kids out to the back yard, motioning to a large dust cloud rising down the gravel road to Chesley's. Under the cloud steadily plodded a large herd of cattle. Andre was yelling "moo, cow, vache, moo, cow, vache!" Vache is French for cow. Poor Mom attempted to make us bilingual by amalgamating baby talk, French and English. As the great dust mushroom grew and the herd rumbled near, the excited cheers reached a fevered pitch, all of us yelling with glee. Suddenly, as the lead animal approached our gate, which except for this time was usually closed, it veered into the openness of our yard, prompting us all to run bumping into each other and screaming in terror to the safety of the house. The farmer was helpless, as the beasts picked up speed, rounding the front of the house then turning toward the back to encircle us completely. We were trapped inside, by a marauding gang of cows. They rounded the house about four or five times and then it was as if someone threw a switch. They all stopped abruptly and wandered around the yard, leisurely nibbling on Memere's freshly mown grass clippings. It didn't take long before the still startled farmer was able to round them all up, forcing the cattle back through the gate and onto the road again to find somebody else to bully.

Uncle Toto wondered about the hoof marks still imprinted in the grass when he arrive the following Sunday. Nobody told him about our uninvited visitors. We just let him scratch his head in wonderment, saving ourselves from weeks of teasing.

I learned many important things during those summers in Petersfield. I learned that skunks can make themselves at home anywhere, there is always an easier way to do things and if you don't care for unexpected visitors, always have your gate closed.

Most importantly, I learned that if you work too many hours, the rest of your life will be spent sleeping.

Auntie Lil

Nick

Auntie Emma, Yvonne, Victor and Andre

# COUNTRY BOYS

In 1944, prior to the end of the war when children in Europe where starving, I was born early one cool September morning. Mom had heard stories about emaciated, tots dying in the normally thriving cities of Germany, Italy and France and Dad had seen the horrors first hand before being wounded and transported home on a hospital ship.

Determined not to have the same thing happen to their precious, they sacrificed their ration coupons to feed me minced bacon and eggs and mashed potatoes before reaching only a few months old. This set a trend that would, before long, produce a rather plump little girl. By the time I reached eleven, Mom had changed her thoughts and began lecturing me on the evils of too many sweets; monitoring everything that passed my lips, at least everything she was able to catch sight of. It must have been extremely frustrating for her, because living in the house with Dad was like residing with the "Great God of Gooey Goodies". After finishing work each day, he took the route home, which passed by "Ye Olde European" bakery. Never did our back door open without his good hand offering a loaf of fresh aromatic bread, the top sprinkled with toasted sesame seeds or flaky apple turnovers injected with whipped cream, which held the highest position on his list of favorites. He too had a problem with his weight, but somehow it never seemed as ugly if a man was of a "generous size".

I don't remember that Mom ever fretted over Dad's girth, she loved him just the way he was. Periodically, he became aware of his chubbiness and tried a few fad diets, one of which was the "Swedish Milk Diet". A tall tin, loosely filled with rustling orange granules came with instructions to mix two heaping tablespoonfuls with an eight-ounce glass of milk and drink twice daily, replacing breakfast and lunch. The stubborn grains never really blended with the milk, most remaining in tact and floating on the surface or clinging to the sides of the glass. Dad never lost much weight and hated the way the little particles stuck in the crevices of his teeth, tinting his toothbrush to a sickening orange color and transforming his usually steely nerves to touchy hot wires. He soon gave up on trying once again to lose weight, reverting to his old carefree self.

With the onset of puberty, my life became filled with half-hearted diets, Midol pills, training bras and the ingestion of hot-pink colored gelatin capsules to encourage strong nails and shiny hair. When fourteen years old, I entered into a self-imposed diet, indulging strictly in only salads, hard-boiled eggs and buttermilk. By the next summer my body had whittled down to that of a fairly decent size 12. Boys were beginning to notice my existence and I was thrilled to hear the shrill wolf whistles from passing cars and the raunchy comments from clutches of young lads gliding past my girlfriends and me on the street or "accidentally" bumping into us in the soda shop. They boosted my confidence and perked an interest in creatures I had only considered to be creeps and the opposition in schoolyard games. The only boys tolerable in my mind up to that time were my little brother Andre and cousins Victor and Phil.

My best friend Linda and I thought we looked so cool in

those wonderful carefree days, with ponytails and pin curls poking out from colored, square scarves tied in knots just under our chins.

Linda and I met our first day in grade nine at St. Mary's Academy. She was small in stature with naturally curly brown hair and wide green eyes. Her eyes watered when she laughed and she had a habit of twisting the curl on her forehead with her finger while reading or pretending to be coy. Unlike me, she brought home some high marks, had a passion for those sappy tragedy songs and overused the word, "doo-hickey. She was quite popular with the sport-jacketed boys from St. Paul's High but I preferred the French fellows from St. Boniface and toughies from the other side of Stafford Street.

Linda lived in River Heights with her wee, frail grandmother, her working mom and twin brother, David. Her father passed away some time before we met but the heartache was evident whenever she mentioned his name; so to ease the pain I often shared my dad with her. On Saturdays, he'd take us for a soda to the Blue Bird Café down the road or across the street to the drugstore lunch counter with its red leather swivel stools and delicious aromas of burgers with greasy, fried onions. Sometimes, when he felt really flush, he bought us each foamy strawberry milk shakes or chocolate malts the consistency of wet cement. Linda would gaze wistfully at Dad and giggle in her unique guttural style, her eyes watering as she whispered in my ear how handsome she thought he was. She wasn't telling me something I didn't already know.

Despite having plenty of my own clothes I preferred to raid Dad's closet pulling out his old white dress shirts, wearing the tails out over blue jeans or pastel pedal pushers. Shirtsleeves and jean bottoms were rolled up and white socks rolled down before Linda and I would put pennies in our loafers or lace up the blue and white saddle shoes and be off to flirt with the boys.

Petersfield holiday summers were no exception. We were eager to find the difference between the city boys and country lads. Phil and Victor had invited a steady stream of handsome young duck-tailed fellows who strutted around without shirts showing off their young pimpled backs and hairless chests. Unfortunately, they were only interested in fishing and most had girlfriends waiting on them in the city. We pretended we didn't care and looked to the abundant supply of what we thought to be less sophisticated country boys.

Petersfield and the surrounding towns and farms were ripe with sixteen and seventeen year-old males as full of the wonderment and excitement in coming of age as we. We had met a few young muscle-boys and Coppertoned kings, but none really fancied us any more than we cared for them. We did however, develop friendships with some fellows like Donny and his brother, Alex who lived in Clandeboye and Larry, whose parents owned Chesley's resort just down the road from our place. The country boys liked to flex their muscles. Alex and the fellow working at the Clandeboye gas station could hold a car high and long enough for someone to change one of the tires.

There didn't seem to be one that wasn't brown-skinned and rippling except, maybe Larry who spent his time boating, fishing and entertaining tourists and vacationers. He had a few cents in his pocket and a nice car, until one evening, we were told, he slammed into a pig wandering down a gravel road. We heard, the pig kept rolling and Larry couldn't stop. After the dust cleared, the pig was dead and Larry's car resembled an accordion. Fortunately, he wasn't injured but it took more than the few cents in his pocket to fix his automobile.

One evening, when Mom and Auntie Emma were clearing dinner dishes and Memere lay crumpled and snoozing in her wicker rocker, there came the roaring sound of a mufflerless motor. It was speeding down the gravel road from Chesley's resort, followed by a plume of white dust rolling across the field of corn just opposite our place. A beat up red shell of a car turned into our yard, through the old wooden gate, and down the long grassy driveway where it stopped halfway to the house. Donny had brought a young man named Lyle to meet Linda and me. He was tall and handsome, with golden brown skin and his head was crowned with unruly flaxen curls and a filter-less cigarette was perched behind his right ear. Blond whiskers poked from the square jaw and his face brightened with white pearly teeth when he smiled. Immediately, I knew this holiday would be different from all the other years at Petersfield.

Now, I fell in love with every boy that flirted with me and my thoughts were always saturated with the romance of screen stars and recording artists. Knowing all of this was only puppy love; I still enjoyed every exciting minute of it. Fifteen year-old girls are usually too self absorbed to be hurt by anyone except maybe female peers.

I attended high-school classes at St. Mary's Academy girls' school where there was never a shortage of primping, preening and sharp-tongued gossip. I was the butt of fat jokes all through elementary school, so by the time I was a senior at St. Mary's, my shell was bulletproof and very little damaged my confidence, determining me to leave such misery behind. And so it was, I had a whole summer of country music, long kisses and released emotions ahead of me. Never having experienced the pain of a broken heart, there were no hurtful memories in my mind to hold me back from placing my young heart into the callused hands of this sweet country boy.

We told Nick, Auntie's boyfriend, to inform Mom we had gone for a ride with friends. The poor naïve soul was reprimanded sternly by three screaming women for letting us fly away with virtual strangers. Mom had spent far too much time with Linda and me not to know how harebrained we both were and I suspect her own youthful experiences became suddenly fresh in her mind to heighten her apprehensions.

Lyle worked at a stone quarry in another village, but had most evenings and a few afternoons off. The four of us watched the sunsets over golden fields and attended after-hours dances at Crabby Steve's barn. We rambled under the sunshine, down dusty gravel roads, stopping to smell wild roses and pick bull rushes growing in ditches. Lazy summer hours were consumed resting in tall grasses, melting into nature, lying still to eavesdrop on bird songs and watch the colorful, jittery butterflies. Sometimes, we'd pick corn from patches of tall whispering stalks, eating them raw and laughing at the kernels stuck in each other's teeth.

The less traveled, back road to Winnipeg Beach was our favorite, the two narrow ruts directing us along farmers' hayfields where the marsh came in to meet the road in places, offering us glimpses of possum and skunk gathering fishy morsels to feed hungry youngsters hiding in the high grasses. Cellophane-winged dragonflies of cherry and blue filled the air above and the ground oozed green with reeds and marsh grasses pushing through the mossy surface and waving on warm, earthy-smelling country breezes.

Winnipeg Beach, in the 1960's was a magnet for teenagers, country and city alike. The boardwalk beckoned with flashing lights, bumpy rides and bubbling music outpouring from every attraction. The aroma of succulent hot dogs, sweet cotton candy and french fries flooded our noses and lured us to the chip wagons and small greasy cafes on sultry fish-fly kinds of nights. Hours were spent monopolizing restaurant tables while listening to juke box tunes, sipping frosty colas and loosening saltshaker lids. It was usually warm in the diners despite the many screened windows and the fans pushing the moist, heavy air around. It seemed there was always at least one neon light flickering and buzzing along with the multitude of flies pestering patrons or stuck to the tacky paper traps hanging in spirals from the ceilings. Occasionally, we would meet some of Lyle and Donny's friends. The boys were always amiable, the girls not usually. They would serve us sideways glances and whisper, then giggle to each other, endeavoring to make us feel uneasy. It never worked, as we were unaware of any personal flaws and were too cool to admit it if there were.

I always loved to walk the Winnipeg Beach shoreline at night. On windy evenings, often when a storm was imminent, the waves crashed on the sparkling sand and white caps winked in the black expanse of water. We young lovers would shed our shoes, roll up pant legs and wade in the warm water, spilling out our dreams and aspirations and sharing lofty hopes for our futures. We'd hold on to each other as watery fingers pulled at our feet and the sand fell away from under our toes. It was then I wish time could have stood still. It was then, that we had nothing blocking our way and fueled by the exuberance of youth, we pushed on. We never realized how perfect life was at that very moment.

I like to believe Lyle and Donny thought of us as special just as we felt about ourselves, but our days together were not always sweet innocence. We were teenagers, no different than kids of today and dangerous excitement was a craving not one of us denied ourselves. We were stupid and determined fearless, knowing a higher power was self-appointed to watch over us. We sped down the highways, the frame of the old jalopy creaking from the push of the wind, as we encouraged Donny's little transistor radio to barely be heard above the roar in our ears from the gusts deflected by the windshield streaming over to buffet our sun-streaked hair. We played with fire; bumping kerosene flares set out to warn of road construction barriers. The little metal orbs would roll under the car to the side of the road, resting in the grass or being snuffed out by dark, watery ditches. Accelerating down the highway, the boys once recognized a peer walking on the loose gravel, shoulder. As we approached, Lyle drove close and Donny opened the rear door endeavoring to bump the hapless soul into the ditch. They carried out the maneuver with such deftness, I am sure they must have done it before, and to this day, it gives me chills to think what could have been the consequences of such recklessness.

One dark starry night, we were breezing down the winding road around Chesley's resort in the old red clunker, when along a sharp turn, the left side back door flung open, propelling Linda out of the car and down the incline to the creek. Lyle screeched to a stop, vaulting from the car to fetch Linda from the shining oil-slicked water near the launching dock. She looked like a sheep's behind; her naturally curly hair tightened to sopping, tight coils and her face streaked from the liberal coating of black mascara on her thick, upturned eyelashes. The seat of her pants was caked with stinky wet mud and once again, despite her embarrassment, we considered the whole episode a big adventure. We did however, think it unfortunate that the luster wore from the event upon our return to the house where we had some elaborate explaining to appease Mom and Memere. Of course Auntie Emma, in her own wisdom, found it just as humorous as we.

Down the yellow, gravel road east of our place was Gilbert's. Chesley's was on one end of the road running behind our house and Gilbert's was at the other. I recall being told it was there even before Mr. Skinner, Pepere's neighbor, moved into the quaint house that sat beside the little inlet just west of us. He was there from my very first recollections of Petersfeild Sunday excursions to visit Pepere, when we arrived in Alex's big, black 1949 Oldsmobile or Nana and Grandpa Sharpe's little Austin. Mr. Skinner sold hotdogs from a stand he erected during earlier days in the town of Lockport, south of Petersfield. His stand became very popular and grew to fit its popularity. When we patronized the place, ample hamburgers, French fries, sodas in glass bottles and crunchy-skinned, smoked hotdogs were the favorites ordered from the limited menu. Young people flocked to Skinners to eat, drink and listen to the latest, rock&roll songs belting out from the jukeboxes and speakers outside. There was a big room, crammed with pinball machines, challenging the wizards of the day and the walls of the restaurant were lined with black and white photos of hockey heroes. There was an atmosphere there, as with many eateries of it's kind in the 1960's that is now gone. On warm humid evenings, the spacious parking lot was a buzz with teens from the city as well as the surrounding countryside. You could always depend on witnessing the odd hormone-fuelled fight in that parking lot and expect to stumble over young couples necking on the grass along the Red River that pulsed past Skinners and through the locks to Lake Winnipeg.

When Linda and I spent our summer together at Petersfield, Gilbert's was sold to another family concern. The name at the property entrance was changed to read, "Cameron's." A leafy shaded lane opened on a clearing, presenting an office and snack bar perched on a piece of land that jutted out to the mouth of the channel. Being closer to the marsh than any of our places, Cameron's property supported more wildlife. It was not unusual to see multi-colored wood ducks or tall, thin-legged cranes fishing for food in the shallow, algae-crusted water near the shore. Poking out from a stretch of tall ruffed bank was a pipe supplying a steady stream of delicious, cold water pouring like liquid silver from an artesian well which was buried somewhere below in the cool earth. One time Linda and I over-indulged ourselves, drinking far too much of the clear, sparkling water. We paid for it by spending a miserable evening jostling for space in the little green outhouse. Dad said our bodies weren't used to the minerals in the country water. From that day on, we only drank the stale stuff Mom lugged from the city in her collection of Javex jugs occupying a goodly sized space on the floor, in the musty dark at the bottom of the basement stairs.

Some Petersfield mornings were warm and dry, making me feel as if I had not slept at all. Stifling heat has always made my eyes feel scratchy and takes the breath from me. I held a strong dislike for those mornings, knowing that it would only get hotter as the days wore on. The heat never seemed to bother Memere. She would waste a great deal of her breath trying to convince us kids that hard work in the blazing sun baked our skin to a lovely golden brown and was a wonderful source of vitamin C. We preferred to escape to the cool leafy orchard, indulging in sweet ripe plums and tart crab apples or to the old barn with its dim unexplored corners.

Thankfully, most Petersfield mornings were cool and misty, with wet grass under bare feet, and the creek usually calm with just a few ripples from circling water beetles and bubbles surfacing from crayfish resting in the silky mud bottom. Fishing was best on those mornings. I'd cast my line out over the polished green stillness, the weight breaking the water with a resounding plunk. I'd sit cross-legged on the dock, one finger on the line, dreaming of romance and the time when the old red jalopy would once again turn into our yard.

As August waned and September approached, it was time to bid the summer farewell. The structure of fall and the winter to follow, awaited our little Petersfield family. The hotel beckoned to Memere, with its paperwork, famil-iar patrons and salesmen and barroom smells. She was refreshed and ready to deal with business associates and play bingo with her friends.

The P.T.A. and home fires called to Mom. She missed the colorful noisy traffic whizzing around our corner house and the phone calls with news of neighborhood goings-on.

Auntie's Avon customers were awaiting her return. Back orders were piling up and deliveries had to be made around town. She had customers all over the city and spent many hours traveling by transit to drop off orders and pamphlets for future sales.

My cousins and brother as well as Linda and I, were anticipating another school year with summer stories to share with missed friends. It was time to say good-bye to the country boys and get back to school dances and burg-ers at the "Dubs" and Pony Corral.

My summer fling had come to an end and the dilemma of trying to deal with a city-country romance was ahead of me. The city was my more constant existence, it held the people I planned to carry with me through the end of my life. I nursed dreams of graduating with my friends, be-coming gainfully employed and irresponsibly flying off to the taste the pleasures of the world. At sixteen, a steady boyfriend was not part of my plan. The novelty of the sum-mer soon wore off for Lyle, as cold, highway trips to the city in the dead of winter became tedious and the three-year difference in our ages became an issue.

Lyle gave me an exciting summer filled with tender experiences and fun and for that, to him I am thankful. These memories are now tucked away deep in my heart and sleep hidden in the bottom of my old photo box.

Those wonderful, carefree days at Petersfield taught me many things. Old people must not feel the heat, one should tighten saltshaker lids before using and always check the road for pigs when joy riding.

Most importantly, just because your Mom and Dad think you are wonderful and will love you forever does not mean that every one else in the world will.

Country Boys

# A POCKET FULL OF GIGGLES

Cousin Yvonne was a couple of years younger and at one time shorter than I. Her adolescent chubbiness was a source for teasing as well as the thick, wing-framed eye-glasses and a face puffed with rosy cheeks full of uncontrollable giggles. Despite being painfully shy, she was always game for anything. Bravery was instilled deep in her little soul and she could be talked into participating in all my stupid antics, sharing in the punishments when we were caught in the acts.

Yvonne spent a few years attending a French Catholic girls school in St. Boniface where she was a boarder; living, eating and sleeping in the company of nuns all week, only to be released on weekends, holy days and holidays. Yvonne dreaded Sunday evenings. As the weekends came to a close, tension would build in the big ancestral home on Luxton Avenue. Painful tears were shed among pleas and tantrums, but she was nevertheless restrained and delivered to the strict, flavorless institution. With time, the adjustment of conforming became less prickly, strong bonds were established and solid friendships made with a few of her peers but still, she pined for the weekends and especially summer holidays.

Vacations at Petersfield were a chance for Yvonne to let her giggles ring free and shed the drab gray uniform for her navy blue swimsuit with what Mom and Auntie called the "flattering skirt", hot pink  pedal pushers and a most unflattering straw hat. These unusual "chapeaus" were the rage only in our little Petersfield world. I never saw anyone else outside of our clan wearing them and do not know where they were purchased. Memere delighted in them, making many her own, sharing the hats with Mom, Auntie and of course Yvonne. I graciously refused when offered, my face flushing with embarrassment at just the thought of anyone seeing me with this oddity perched on my carefully back-combed bouffant do and bobby-pinned kiss-curls. The hats were loosely woven with soft yellow straw and if worn long enough took on a character of their own. Yvonne's choice was a round flat-topped little number with a small brim. She wore it day and night to insure the boys wouldn't hide it on her. Despite her vigilance, there were times when Vic and Phil happened upon the unattended little ditty, tossing it to each other above everyone's heads but mostly, they sat on it and deliberately passed gas which added to the already present "bouquet". With two older brothers, Yvonne was always being tickled, poked at and of course teased  with their "poo-poo, ca-ca" jokes. In my more righteous moments, I took it upon myself to try and insulate her from some of the bullying by dragging her along everywhere with me, whether she wanted to come or not. Many hours were spent  together in the smelly old wooden fishing boat, never going very far, just to the mouth of the channel which was a little past Gilbert's landing. The motor often conked out with a sputter and cloud of blue smoke and we'd have to paddle back as I sometimes couldn't restart it. Most times it did come back to life as I'd tell Yvonne to pray while I pulled at the cord on the rusty old gas guzzler. I figured she had more influence with God since she spent so much time with nuns. The odd afternoon, we would venture into the quiet mossy channel, but only when I had confidence that Yvonne was in a good prayer mode. The channel started out in the marsh, resembling a long corridor with walls of tall, golden and green reeds on each side. Further down toward the lake, there were a few trees and bushes, some with exposed roots fingering ripples into the water. It was usually quiet there, save for the water lapping against the shore and the ever present sounds of gold finches, loons and buzzing great horseflies. When heading down the channel, I would pretend to be in the everglades or down in the Bayou, like the places I'd only seen in black and white on television and dreamed someday of seeing for real, in full color.

Around 1959, all of us kids, except little Andre, moved from our mothers big bedrooms on the main level to two of the three smaller bedrooms upstairs. The house was a story and a half and the eaves were not insulated, just bare unpainted wooden beams and boards with exposed nail heads and a few inhabited spider webs. On most sunny days it was like an oven up there, roasting anything that didn't move. At night, everything moved. The stagnant, warm air was thick with what Mom called "miller moths". Now, teenagers have a tendency to be intense in everything they say and feel and we girls were no exception. I, and especially young Yvonne would become overly agitated when having to deal with anything that had feelers and more than four legs so, every night Mom and Auntie would march upstairs to wage war on the "miller moths". They were armed with pump action glass insect spray bottles and fly swatters crusted with the crushed bodies of bluebottles and horse flies. Yvonne and I would listen to the commotion from the safe zone downstairs, not daring to even peek into the bare, knotty pine stairway leading to the upper level. By the time we went to bed, the air was clear and only a few millers were left, twitching in the corners of our bedroom or in that gap between the screen and the window sill. We drifted off to sleep content in the knowledge that no insect would be dallying with our exposed body parts while we slumbered. Yvonne and I slept in one room and the boys in the other. When Linda came to Petersfield, the three of us shared the bed. The old iron thing we called our bed was not unlike the one in the boys room. Painted a putrid color of brown, it was big enough for a full platoon and complained loudly with every movement we made. Yvonne was a deep, but restless sleeper. She roamed around the large, squeaky bed every night, arms outstretched over our necks and fingers up our noses. After a while, I didn't even find it at all unusual to awaken with Yvonne's odorous little feet on the pillow beside my head.

It was double the fun teasing and pulling pranks on Yvonne because her reaction was always so full. She laughed and giggled, her cheeks instantly turning red with embarrassment or cried when the jokes were pushed to the limit by her brothers. I must admit that I was also, sometimes guilty of taking advantage of her vulnerability. One warm starry night my friend Garnet was visiting and while we were lazing in the back yard, inhaling the clean cool Petersfield air, Yvonne wandered out to use the backhouse. She was completely oblivious to our presence as we purposely remained as quiet as bare feet on silk. When we figured she was settled, Garnet picked an ample-sized rock from the pile at the side of the house and heaved it at the little green structure. Yvonne shot from the outhouse in a panic, her eyes wide with confusion as she padded along the path, adjusting her pajamas and muttering all the way to the safety of the porch. Only seconds later, Auntie Emma exited the house, vigorously slamming the screen door behind her. She did her best to reprimand us, but we could tell, she thought it was funny too.

When I was younger, I hated using the outhouse. The flies and especially the spiders made me very nervous. I usually used the chamber pot in the closet in Mom's bedroom. When sitting there, especially at night, one would have a tendency to doze off. The closet was a warm secure place, filled with Mom's clothes, all perfumed and smelling like her. I didn't mind pooping in the closet at all especially since there were no hairy or winged insects to torment me. One Sunday morning at church, Mom , slowly giving in to the sultry heat and bored with the sermon, bowed her head feigning reverence. While contemplating the white design on her gray, Sunday-go-to-mass dress, she noticed another design, a crusty-looking brown one. She picked at it and it came off in her hands. While performing bodily functions in the closet one night, her dress must have accidentally come between me and the toilet paper. She was so embarrassed, she didn't know what to do. Here she was, sitting in a pew with brown crusties on the hem of her dress, crowded on both sides and front and back by strangers in their Sunday best. She discreetly gathered the offending section of cloth so as to sit on it, hoping all the while, we kids would not notice. We giggled at anything in church and she knew this discovery would surely render us uncontrollable. Mom was always the last to leave and this day was no different. As the heat had melted the offending matter, she left the pew and dared not look back. This too was another one of those stories seldom recounted, only coming to light in later years when memories were shared with others.

Yvonne, Andre and I spent many happy hours at Chesley's resort. On lazy warm afternoons we'd meander down the gravel road, stopping while Andre examined frogs and insects or picked colorful wild flowers for Mom, from the ditches beside the road. We would cross the small, gravel topped parking lot in front of the store to the quaint shop which was typical of the 1960's family establishments. Mrs. Chesley presided over the adding machine and till on the small , wooden counter and sold souvenirs and penny candies from the large glass jars on the shelf behind her. We always stopped there first, listening to the juke box in the attached clubroom while we made our choice of candies. The black balls were Andre's favorites. He would always be taking them out of his mouth to see what color they had turned. Yvonne liked the jaw-breaker bubble gum. She would roll the wad of gum around in her mouth, trying in vain to blow a bubble. My favorites were the oversized red, wax lips. It was a dilemma for me to chose whether to wear them or chew them. I liked to think they made me look like a sexy movie star but they also appealed to my taste buds. I would slowly chew off the bits on the inside, the ones that didn't show but then I'd soon break down and chew the whole thing, the flavor only lasting a minute. I was always left with a useless little ball of wax but was never discouraged from buying them again. When our money was spent, we'd walk  out under the welcoming arch to the boathouse and drab gray docks, our little bags of candy in hand. Every once in a while, a large luxury boat came in and was anchored just out past the maze of bobbing docks. We would sit cross-legged on the splintered boards of the old pier, carefully avoiding the dried out minnows and worms left by disgruntled fishermen. The candy was traded and dreams were shared about where we would go if one of those wonderful yachts were ours. One cool and rainy day, a small replica of an old pirate ship was resting in the still waters in front of Chesley's. It had to have come from the channel, slipping by us in the dark of night. We could see it from our place if we stood on the dock and looked west. Andre wasted no time running down to Chesley's, hoping to catch a glimpse of Captain Hook, or maybe Black Beard.

One would think that damp rainy days at Petersfield would have been miserable. Five cooped up kids and three women are not what one would consider and ideal situation for calm, but surprisingly it was. Auntie's closet, besides housing  Sunday clothes and the chamber pot, was home to a big cardboard box filled with comic books. Our boys would get lost for hours flying through the skies with superman or taming the Wild West along side Wild Bill Hickock. Mom would do the mending and Memere snoozed the day away in her, creaky, old, wicker chair. Memere was not noted for her domestic abilities. Cooking and sewing did not come as natural to her as did business ventures so she would bring a large sack of her mending and altering work to Petersfield for Mother to deal with. Mom spent many hours replacing elastics in bloomers and refashioning modern brassieres to resemble the flat, curve-less ones worn at the turn of the century. Memere was a modern, 1950's woman on the outside and a 1900's woman underneath. We all favored certain styles and I suppose Memere's was the cut of her underwear. Auntie Emma spent her rainy days painting her tapered fingernails red and writing to her sister-in-law  Simone who resided in Edmonton. Auntie Simone joined us one year at Petersfield and was delighted to add her posterior to our rosary circle as we kneeled with our faces bowed to the backs of the chairs and sofas lining the living room. She understood French. The locals at St. Anne's Church that Sunday weren't in the least bit surprised to see Auntie Simone emerge from the back of Nick's old truck. I guess they were getting used to us.

Yvonne and I spent hours lazing on Auntie's big quilted

bed, reading her romance magazines when we weren't up-stairs in Nick's room. Sometimes, we'd sneak up there to thumb through the girlie magazines he kept hidden under his mattress. I wonder if the boys knew they were there or if Nick ever suspected the invasion of his privacy when thumbing through the dog-eared pages. With that many kids around, nothing was private.

Unlike today, back on our summers with Memere, we usually stopped what we were doing to look up and see who was going by on the creek. The water was always quiet, save for the odd summer soul out for a scenic boat ride or Mr. Chesley in his green minnow boat with the net in front, gathering bait for the weekend rush. We could usually tell who it was by the color of the boat or the tilt of the hat. The end of the week would bring a few more people, mostly working daddies who would take the kids for rides to the lake or up and down the creek on water skis. Come Monday, everything would be serene again, with just the call of the loons in the early morning mist and the melodic songs of brightly colored country birds ser-enading us through the rest of the day.

One evening, a great huge owl decided to roost on the roof of our outhouse which really rattled poor Auntie Emma who had a phobia for birds. When she wandered out that night to use the facilities, she had a feeling of be-ing watched. As she approached the door, there was a slight rustling sound and a low whispering, "hooot, hooot." Pointing the flashlight beam upward, she was faced with big golden and black eyes, framed with white feathers and possessing a fearsomely hooked, yellow beak. We were all jolted to our feet by her blood-chilling scream followed only seconds by the porch screen door slamming. Auntie bustled through the living room doorway, white as a sheet, mumbling something about a feathered monster and the outhouse. We tried in vain to remove the creature from his perch. We thought surely it would leave if the big yard flood light were turned on or if we made scary noises. Nothing flustered that big old bird, he was obviously not afraid of anything, let alone a bunch of idiots yelling and one bright light. Consequently, the owl stayed the night on top of our outhouse and Auntie had to use the chamber pot that night, the one she kept in her bedroom closet.

Yvonne never really grew out of her shyness, even through rebellious teenaged years and into young adulthood. She always had an air of uncertainness about her.

Surprisingly though, Yvonne earned her driving license with very little effort at all. Her first car was a yellow number we called "Lemon Drop". She chauffeured Auntie Emma around town, delivering Avon orders and waiting patiently while Auntie rode the elevators in downtown office buildings and banks, dropping off brochures and filling out order slips.

Some Saturdays, Yvonne would drive from the North End to meet me in one of the South End pubs we found amusing where we'd spend afternoons, draped over chairs, while drinking 25 cent glasses of draft and pretending we didn't notice the fellows smiling from the next table.

I became the privileged one to accompany Yvonne on her first highway driving experience. Of course, we chose highway #9 to Petersfield, fearlessly planning this whole new adventure. We talked of the freedom of the open road as we traveled through the city pointing north toward wide open spaces. I have experienced some pretty unsettling things and this one sits very near the top of the list.

As the panorama of green and blue farmers' fields stretch ahead of us, the ribbon of gray, the road to Petersfield, turned Yvonne into someone I had never met before. Her hands gripped the wheel with white-knuckle determination as her foot pressed hard on the gas pedal, propelling the Lemon Drop to speeds I had never before experienced. She managed to push that little Valliant so close to the cars ahead of us, I could smell the exhaust and then she quickly darted into the passing lane, only to shoot back with inches to spare ahead of the car we had just passed. I ignored the wide eyes and twisted faces of the drivers in the automobiles falling behind us and tried not to think about what may lay on the road ahead. With the turn to Petersfield eminent, Yvonne eased up on the gas, transferring her heavy foot to the brakes, which whined and squealed off the highway on to the loose gravel of the little country road. At this point, the car slowed to a crawl as Yvonne reverted to the cousin I knew so well, the shy and quiet gentle one.

We enjoyed a wonderful peaceful day in the shadow of the old insilbrick, feasting on the tasty morsels Auntie had packed for us and resting our bodies in the warm country sunshine. The morning quickly melted into late afternoon and it was time to hit the road, time for another one of Miss Toad's wild rides. The drive home was just as harrowing as the one going to Petersfield. Yvonne left a string of shaken drivers in her wake, passing at high speeds and seemingly taking curves on two wheels. By the time we arrived to the safety of the city I was reduced to a cowering piece of my normally carefree self. This time it was me who was reciting the Hail Marys. Yvonne just looked over to me and giggled in that shy innocent way of hers. Who knew?

I learned many things from those days in Petersfield with Yvonne. I learned that chamber pots should never be kept in clothes closets, big owls can sit wherever they please and you never really know someone till you drive with them.

Most importantly, I learned that pure prayer can bring anything to actuality, it can even restart a stalled, rusted outboard motor.

# DARK NIGHTS

I don't remember anything quite so black as a moonless Petersfield night. The suffocating stillness was enough to bring anxiety to anyone's soul, even the adults seasoned by many dark nights and having long out-grown the bogeyman. When the wind died in the evening, and the darkness snuffed out the sparkle on the creek, we children felt there was a presence of someone other than the members of our little Petersfield clan. The profusion of stars creeping about the sky didn't even send the least little glimmer of light to relieve the niggling in our spines. Some of us enjoyed that sensation, some of us didn't.

My young brother, Andre enjoyed anything that added color to his already vibrant imagination. Even at six or seven years old, the muted colors of night blended well in his love of the things that brought uneasiness to most of us. Linda and I tried our best to scare him and Yvonne, telling them stories of smelly zombies and unholy ghosts wandering aimlessly in the darkness of the backyard hoping to bump into a young tender morsel on their way to the outhouse. Yvonne's eyes would grow large and white as she fidgeted uncomfortably in her seat or squeezed herself down into her favorite musty old stuffed chair in the front room. Not Andre, he always begged for more, asking us to tell him again about the spirit who seeped through the

94

crack between the door and the floor; "the one that comes and sits on your chest while you are sleeping", he would ask, his face poised with eyebrows arched in anticipation.

Phil always tried his best to be the "cool cat", the one that could deal with any situation in a nonchalant manner. Linda and I enjoyed luring him to the back yard after the sun melted down and a cool dew settled on the lawn. We'd sit in a close bunch on the big blue blanket, munching on our well earned chocolates and potato chips, marveling at blinking fire-flies and vocalizing our wishes for the future. Phil was a scrappy hockey player, but could play like a pro and hoped someday to make it to the big leagues. Linda planned on studying nursing and I just wanted to leave school behind as quickly as possible as I was not much of a student   Most of my school hours were spent gazing from classroom windows, my mind entertaining thoughts of carelessly traveling the world. Poor Phil  was eventually lulled into a sense of security by our twittering on about frivolous things and colorful subjects like movie stars and the latest fashions. Our conversations would be suddenly interrupted to point out a movement near the old barn, barely visible from the dim glow of the house windows or the strange shape of a large tree suddenly moving on a breathless night. Then there were the sounds, "did you hear that?' Linda would innocently ask with a little cringe in her voice. It wasn't long before Phil devised an elaborate but lame excuse and retreated to the soft lights and security of the house. Some other nights he would join us in the moonless outdoors, confident in his renewed bravery, but he seldom managed any longevity.

Now nothing bothered Victor, or at least he never let us know if anything did. He was the old one, a couple of physical years past Phil and I, and fifty years ahead of us in mind and soul. He was the serious one, his pensiveness usually affirmed by a deeply furrowed forehead. He was honestly instilled with the belief that we, the younger creatures, were deposited on this earth to be a burden to him, always bringing something stupid to his normally ordered life. Our ignorance did however, provide him with hours of nettling power, meshing his little barbs into popular Johnny Cash songs. We had to endure his torturous vocalizing because there was no way ever to stop him once he got started on what he thought an appropriate tune. Even Auntie Emma's wrath did not scare him. He sang loud and long, his whining voice piercing every peaceful corner of the property, finding and offending our ears no matter where we chose to hide. Needless to say, no ghost stories ever bothered him.

Surprisingly, stormy rainy days at Petersfield were rather nice. They would bring us all together in the living-room to play cards or just laze deep in the big furniture listening to music. As the gloom hung from the skies outside in the heavy lush green, the house would be warm from the glowing hot, wood stove. The coziness always brightly lit our laughter and peppered our conversations. Auntie would prod us to sing along with the strains of popular songs stretching into the living-room from the sputtering little kitchen radio. Her eyes would sparkle as she swayed and clapped along with us and her thoughts probably in reminiscence of her youth. She related well to young people. Her home in Winnipeg always abuzz with the comings and goings of old and young alike. The coffee pot was always on the stove and hospitality, the rule of the day. The same held true for Petersfield. We were seldom without guests while there.

My friend, Garnet, would come most evenings and pick up Linda and me in his big old blue truck. He'd drive us down all the bumpy little back roads, kind of a local tour.

He told us stories about the people who lived in old ram-shackle houses in the bush or about the ones who worked and lived on orderly and expansive, prosperous farms. Garnet pointed out all the good fishing spots and places where native peoples camped in villages along the creek  long before Petersfield was Petersfield. We'd spend many evenings just sitting out in the back yard on the blue blanket, spying on nocturnal animals going about their business in the dark. There were often families of skunk waddling with a seemingly awkwardly gait, gathering the fish guts and skins Auntie Emma left by the banks of the night-quiet creek. The section of Netley Creek that passed by our place was usually quiet except for the vigorous waves created by powerful motorboats knifing their way through the water, most probably on their way to nowhere. Speed then, as it is today romanced many a soul on the water and I must admit, I never turned down the opportunity to accompany some young man in his fiberglass super-boat. The smell of cool river spray and the wind pushing on my face and fingering through my hair certainly aroused feelings in me I never felt when doing anything else. When it became too dark and spooky, long after Phil retreated to the house, we'd move to Garnet's truck. Garnet preferred the truck to coming into the house or even as far as the porch. Mom and Auntie Emma were inviting enough, but Memere was a strong presence and made the boys who came to visit feel quite uncomfortable. Memere enjoyed making young men feel insecure in her presence. She needled them with personal questions, laughing at  the uneasiness that made them squirm and stammer. Maybe she felt they were too wild, brimming with immature hormones and mouths full of marbles and needed to be controlled. Memere was a mistress of control. She knew just about everything that was going on in the family and you could be sure she had injected her influences in somewhere, insuring things would turn out in her favor and to her satisfaction. And so, we would sit in Garnet's big blue chariot, listening to country music as he told us more fascinating  Petersfield and Netley Creek  stories  from his lengthy repertoire.

Whenever Yvonne and I went for a boat ride on Netley Creek, we always respected the cool sparkling water. I often wondered why it was called a creek. When I think of a creek, a small stream or slow running brook pictures in my mind. Netley Creek is as wide as any river I've seen with a current and undertow just as strong. The current carries the green water through the channel to Lake Winnipeg with mighty strength and purpose. The Lake has been known to boil without warning and tales of lost souls are plentiful. Yvonne couldn't swim and I was no fish so we shuttled around, squatting low in the boat at low speed, Yvonne snug in her inner tube and I, confidently protected by the saints she would call upon to ride with us.

There was a game that many teenagers played on the creek. It was an old game that I recalled my Dad telling us he played when he was young and foolish. It was a very simple and dangerous exercise in attempted heroics followed by humiliation. Usually a couple of fellows took a canoe for a paddle on the creek, deliberately tipping over and pretending to be in distress. The calls for help urged would-be rescuers to come to their aid, only to be laughed at upon their arrival. The boys would flip the canoe to the upright position, hop in and paddle away, thumbing their noses at the well-meaning rescuers. Mom called it "crying wolf". Like most young people, I never considered the consequences of such actions, in fact, I thought it was all quite funny. If I had been an accomplished swimmer and had our old green cargo canoe been lighter, I might have considered playing the prank myself. I'm sure Phil would have joined me as he was always looking to try just about anything.

One warm breezy day, Victor was bunched in the cushioned living room wicker chair he often dragged out to the dock for his comfort while fishing. The red and white float from his line was bobbing in the silvery water when a mustard seed yellow canoe glided by, manned by two lovely girls clad in skimpy bathing suits, their golden skin glistening with sun tan oil. They smiled and giggled at Victor as he squirmed in his seat. All of a sudden the canoe flipped over, spilling the girls screaming and thrashing into the creek. I was sitting in the porch, watching all of this unfold and ran out to see why Victor was not getting the motor boat out to fetch them from the water. He called back to me in disgust, claiming they were probably just fooling around; crying wolf. Seconds later, from the cabin two lots over we heard a motor rumble. It was attached to a powerful sparkling orange and yellow striped speed-boat, manned by a handsome tanned young man with chivalry on his mind. I felt I should maybe throw myself off the dock, but I was too late. He pulled the girls from the water and was away in minutes, dragging the offending canoe behind. We will never know if they were "crying wolf" or not. One thing I know for sure, the laugh was on Victor for a change and it was our turn to tease.

There was a very hot July day one summer and everyone was trying to escape the merciless sun. Mom, Andre and Auntie were shelling sweet emerald peas in the shady porch while sipping iced lemonade and Memere was snoozing in her room, of which the shades were drawn. I never saw the inside of Memere's room during all those summers in Petersfield. The blinds were always pulled down fully, so I couldn't even peek in from the outside. It was so dark in there, I felt it held secrets, spooky secrets, most of which I wanted to know nothing. The only thing that did interest me, was where Memere kept all those old boxes of chocolates and bags of stale potato chips we worked so hard to procure. I would like to have seen them all together in a pile, rather than in pieces doled out at the end of the day. I wondered if she had an endless supply stashed away under a trap door in the floor of that mysterious room.

It was such a hot dry day, breathing was even difficult. Victor and Phil were sipping Mom's fresh squeezed lemonade while stretched out in the boat somewhere on the creek. Fishing was their excuse for such leisure while seeking shade under their big woven straw sombreros which were souvenirs Auntie bought for them while on vacation in Mexico. Yvonne and I wandered down the lane, under lifelessly still trees, past vacationers lazing in patio chairs on the patchy, parched lawns. We waved to our neighbors between our place and Chesley's, commenting on how good their places looked and asking if they were well.

Chesley's resort consisted of a store, restaurant and clubroom, situated on a large expanse of land, where the road made a forty-five degree angle, continued past our place and ended up at Gilbert's resort. On the creek side was a maze of docks, a landing area and a rather crude boat house. Cabins and trailers dotted the property, each usually filled with vacationers getting away from the city summer heat.

This day was a scorcher and the only relief we could think of was to get to Chesley's for some ice-cream or a cold cola from the gurgling chest cooler in the clubroom. If you put a nickel in the sliver slot and opened the lid, the metal teeth in the cooler would release, offering a cool bottle from the watery bottom. The fans in the clubroom were just serving to circulate the hot air and the flies were sticking, so we sauntered outside with thoughts of dipping our burning feet in the cool water from the avenue of docks on the beachfront. Just the thought of cooling our feet made us feel better.

The swimming area was full of small children and adults, all endeavoring to lower body temperatures. The level of noise and activity proved the refreshing water was providing the relief intended. Children ran in and out of the sand-churned shoreline water, sporting water wings and bouncing colorful beach balls to their parents, showing only shoulders and white rubber bathing caps above the green, murky surface.

We noticed two boisterous young men out beyond the docks in a canoe, as we hung around the boathouse talking to Mr. Chesley. He would work, sanding and painting his boats while listening to us and pretending to be interested. The two fellows on the creek were playing that stupid tip-your-canoe game. They were calling for help and everyone was laughing and yelling back, much to the R.C.M.P. officer's alarm. He had just pulled his official car into the parking lot and wandered down to the docks chugging on an icy Kik cola he had just picked up at the club room. He was visibly upset and asked some people to boat him out to rescue the drowning duo but one fellow explained that it was just a silly game, one the two brothers played all the time. Then everyone became quiet, something didn't seem right. One boy was now alone in the water and the canoe was following the current down the creek. The smooth water paved over where the other boy should have been. The police officer ran back to his car to call for backup and the water was dragged in the remains of the day and that night in hopes of recovering the young man's body. I never knew if it was found, as Dad and Alec came to take us home to Winnipeg the next day.

"Crying wolf" had been played once too often and now the consequences were sadly realized. The summer ended on a sour note and there was one less fresh face in senior high that year.

I read somewhere that Petersfield was originally named St. Louis and Netley Creek, Death River. It seems two aboriginal tribes were wiped out by disease while living on the banks of the river, long before that young man's spirit joined them in the history of Netley Creek.

I learned many things during those summers at Petersfield. I learned that you should never "cry wolf", an old woman can easily scare young men and there is more than one way to ruin a good Johnny Cash song.

Most importantly, I learned that you can't tell what a person is really like just by looking at them. The best way to get to know someone is to hold a conversation in the dark.

# DOUGHNUT MAN

Auntie Emma's boyfriend Nick was rough around the edges and smooth at the same time. When I picture him during those summers at Petersfield, I can see a square muscular man whom time had softened a bit. His arms and broad back were still bound with the bulbous muscles of his earlier years but the belly had now begun to slip over the ample belted waist, his forehead was etched the folds and crevices that come with hard living and his chin was in the process of doubling. He spent most Petersfield holidays in the sun, slathered with baby oil, baking his leathered skin and looking somewhat like a well-done Thanksgiving turkey, just out of the oven. Perpetually crinkled eyes sparkled from his weathered face when he smiled and he possessed a voice that was ever so small for such a large presence.

Nick met Auntie in 1951 and by the time we started spending summers at Petersfield, he was well integrated into the family. It was seldom we saw Auntie and her brood without Nick. He ferried them around in his milky sea green cargo van to family dinners, funerals and weddings. He was considered by all of us to be quite permanent although most of us knew Auntie had other fleeting suitors, which she kept secret from Nick, as he certainly would not have understood.

Nick worked as a deliveryman for a bakery in the North End of Winnipeg. When not transporting kids, the old van was filled with doughnuts for stores and cafeteria coffee breaks.

One day, he decided to come out to Petersfield and have an early breakfast with us before starting work. He loaded the doughnuts, checked his change box and headed down the highway in the fresh morning air. He turned onto the Petersfield gravel road before realizing it was being graded. The truck's tires became positioned, one on each side of a high ridge of stones in the middle of the road and jagged rocks and pebbles rubbed against the cumbersome vehicle's undercarriage, creating a terrible racket. To save further damage, Nick decided to gun the motor and at the same time, turn the steering wheel to the right, which he thought would carry him over the ridge on to a more even plane. The loose gravel gave under the wheels, propelling the truck onto the shoulder, into the air and then down into the ditch, spinning it over and over again. The rear doors flew open, shattering the windows and spewing doughnuts and money like confetti into the clear country air, before the battered vehicle came to rest on its four flattened tires.

As the smoke dissipated and the dust settled, Nick, a little beaten and bruised, sat stunned, still in the driver's seat. He gathered his thoughts and eventually eased his then, aching body out of the bent frame to survey the damage. He was greeted with the sight of a hundred doughnuts dotting about two hundred feet of marshy ditches and bumpy yellow gravel. Dimes, nickels and quarters winked and glistened on the road from between the loose pebbles in the cool morning sunshine.

Thankful just to be alive, Nick broke into gales of hysterical laughter as, to add insult to injury, a flurry of white gulls appeared, squealing and diving to feast on this banquet so unceremoniously set out before them on the road to Petersfield.

Soon after the doughnut incident, Nick was proud to land a good job as a butcher in a meat packing plant in the east end of the city. His paychecks were much more substantial enabling him to buy a sleek black car to match the prestige that came with his new income. There were no more bumpy rides for us in the back of the truck to the brightly painted white building that was St. Anne's Church on Petersfield Sunday mornings. Instead, we sat piled on each other in the rear seat of Nick's new pride and joy, big kids on the bottom and little ones on top. There were many moans and groans from the inflicting of small bruises caused by sharp elbows, bony bottoms and bickering induced by inappropriate pinching, but nevertheless we were pleased to arrive at church in a vehicle with a little more class than the old panel truck had offered. The locals still stared, but we liked to think they were just in awe of the wonderful car we in which we were riding. We were never short of feeling full of ourselves in those days. One wonders where all this self-confidence flies off to as years go by.

We benefited from Nick's newly acquired position, when he provided much of the meat for our Petersfield table. We dined on delicacies as well as the fine basic cuts of beef. Dinner plates graced with pan-fried, sirloin steak was not an unusual sight on the oil-clothed kitchen table.

We weren't the only ones to partake of this bounty. Nick lived with his elderly mother, one of those sweet old Ukrainian women you might see sitting in the front pew in church, wearing a colorful babushka and fingering an old wooden rosary. She was a fundamental woman, uncomplicated and used to hard work and simple things. They lived in a modest little white house in the north end of the city not far from Auntie Emma.

One day Nick hurriedly delivered a beef tenderloin to his home during the lunch hour in hopes that his mother would broil some of it up for supper that evening. Upon arriving home for his evening repast, a wonderful aroma pulled his nose through the house to the kitchen. His mother was sitting at the table, an empty bowl in front of her and a half eaten morsel of fresh bread in her hand. With a wide loving smile on her face, she smacked her lips and told him he should bring home more of the same kind of meat as this was the best stew she had ever made.

Nick would wander the property at Petersfield bare-backed and wearing worn old cut-offs long before they became fashion. No job was too tough. He was always busy, tilling the garden or clearing deadwood in the orchard. Priding himself on his physical strength, he seldom passed up the opportunity to demonstrate it to us. He organized tugs-of-war, pitting himself against all of us kids, pulling us off our feet with one simple jerk. We complained bitterly but were always begging for "just one more chance" to beat him at his favorite game.

One cool, overcast morning, the boys were given their opportunity to flex their own adolescent muscles. Mr. Scofield, a medium looking man of medium height, came to the house asking assistance from Victor and Philip. He was grazing a small flock of sheep on the lush property just west of ours. I was surprised at how grimy these animals were with their wool dusty gray, rusty in spots and full of burrs. Being a city girl, I had only seen book pictures and dreams in my head of white fluffy lambs. Mr. Scofield needed help to load the sheep onto his truck because they had nibbled all the grass down to the ground and were starting to wander.

Mrs. Veitch resided on the lot, which was green with

low weeping trees and an inlet from the creek that was thick with tall reeds and bull-rushes. The house always looked to me as if it should have been deep in an enchanted forest and made of gingerbread. We trespassed there on occasion, marveling in such wildlife as skunk, raccoon and possums, playing possum.

Being used to the country boys, knowledgeable in animal ways, Mr. Scofield neglected to tell our young men to nab and load the ewes first. Every time they tried to grab one of those cute little lambs, the mother sheep would charge, butting and bumping into soft city bums. Philip enjoyed the adventure immensely. He never minded getting beaten up, just so long as he was having a good time. Victor took the pummeling a little more seriously.

As soon as Mr. Scofield drove away with his bleating cargo, the boys hobbled back to see if Mom's great medicine chest held anything to soothe bumps and scrapes, although the most painful and untreatable injuries were butted behinds. It was suggested, the only remedy would be a cool soak in the creek and Auntie supplied them with a big bar of "Persian Wood", perfumed soap to tame the gaminess that permeated their young hides.

Whenever my cousins and I went swimming off the end of the dock, the soft murky creek bed would churn under our feet, mixing with the clear green water above it. We always emerged with a thin layer of mud clinging to the wispy hair around our mouths and weighing down the seats of our bathing suits. Nick poured buckets of rainwater over our heads and down the backs of bathing suits to loosen the stubborn gelatinous goo. I often wondered how Nick was able to regularly bathe in the creek and exit so squeaky clean. It was probably due to the big bar of Auntie's perfumed soap and wiry scrub brush he took in the creek with him. He employed the same scrub brush,

Mom used to wash the hardwood floors. Billowing suds would surround him as he vigorously scrubbed under his arms and even the soles of his feet, hammertoes wiggling in the air to the rhythms of the Burl Ives tunes he was always singing. Not knowing all the words, he just sang the chorus over and over and over again. He shaved his face clean every day, sometimes in the creek but most mornings from the white, rainwater filled basin. Aromas of bay rum and soap lingered in the air long after he moved to the chores of the day.

Many people sought after Auntie Emma's company. The back door to her city home was always unlocked and the kitchen held the aroma of coffee from the endless pots kept warm on the stove element. Her "office" consisted of a kitchen chair pulled under the end of a huge wooden oil-clothed table; her mail and Avon brochures on one side, her personal cosmetics and coffee cup on the other. She "held court" every day and evening, entertaining customers and friends, old and new, male and female. It was Auntie's male friends Nick's imagination had a problem with. Men always paid attention to Auntie and she enjoyed being noticed, knowing in her heart it was all in fun. Auntie had only one great serious love in her life; her late husband Victor. No one could fill Auntie's heart like he could, not even Nick, not ever.

There was a side of Nick, we as children, seldom witnessed. He sometimes acted irrationally, fuelled by alcohol and the jealousy that lived inside of him. I suppose, in his heart he knew Auntie would never marry him. Words were said in haste and a rift began to widen as time passed and Auntie Emma grew tired of the accusations.

Nick and Auntie parted as the end of the nineteen-sixties approached. Nick married someone else in 1972. His dream of being a successful man were realized when he bought a little grocery store in the North End. He presided over his own meat counter, showcasing an array of fine cuts and his own homemade garlic sausage. Dad, my brother Andre and I visited Nick's shop, shortly after his "grand opening." He led us on a tour of the small establishment, beaming as we expressed our amazement of the walk-in cooler, which housed huge sides of beef hanging to age on big hooks for his special customers.

I was reading the obituaries one September and was met once again, with Nick's sweet smile and crinkled, sparkling eyes. He was almost eighty-seven years old.

I learned many important things those summers at Petersfield with Nick. I learned that seagulls love doughnuts, beef tenderloin makes a fine, succulent stew and no one can remember all the words to a Burl Ives song.

Most importantly, I learned that jealousy is a useless emotion. It is one that can erode clear thoughts into hurtful words, words that can destroy love.

# ELVIS IMPERSONATORS

My teenaged years at Petersfield are the most vivid for me, probably because coming of age and romance are intense in the hearts and minds of most thirteen and fourteen year old girls. The memories continue to burn bright in the remnants left to me by the passing of time and the menopause symptoms that have invaded the part of my brain that is supposed to keep me seeming fairly intelligent.

It was an exciting time for me; everything was new and different, even in Petersfield. The country boys actively courted Linda and me and we loved their attention but also had eyes for the parade of young men cousins Victor and Philip invited out to join in fishing expeditions and to help with Uncle Tommy's elaborate schemes and projects.

One year, it seemed all of a sudden the house was stuffed with gangly male bodies draped over the furniture and crackly, almost ripe voices piercing the peaceful murmurings of the country. Among the contingent of crew cuts and v-neck sweaters were two "Elvis " impersonators, sporting muscles manufactured at the corner gym. They wore blue jeans rolled up at the cuff, motorcycle boots and white t-shirts usually with a pack of Players filterless cigarettes held snugly in one rolled-up short sleeve. Alex was as blonde as Eddy was dark. Their long greasy hair was combed back over their ears and up to a jumble of waves on the top of their slightly swollen heads. Neither was old enough to grow the, then trendy, sideburns but managed a few stray whiskers on the upper lip or chin, which was vainly snipped off with a safety razor every morning in full view of my impressed thirteen-year-old eyes. A couple of strands of Eddie's black hair were always hanging in his face and matched fittingly to his dirty little laugh which always made me feel I had missed something in the conversation and was too embarrassed to admit it. The two cocky young men were confident of their fine physiques, strutting around Petersfield, tanned and shirtless, making the other city boys feel gaunt and pale.

The addition to the young male labour force did not go unnoticed by Uncle Tommy and his perpetually over-stuffed job jar.

Every spring season, the creek would rise from the mountainous, melting snow and ice. As the ground became saturated, the basement filled with water, eroding the walls a little more each year. It was decided, by the knowledge-able men in the family, that a five-foot deep trench should be dug to expose the north wall of the foundation. Then the plan was to repair and tar the crumbling cement from the outside, meeting the water before it had a chance to penetrate the vulnerable walls. Uncle Tommy brought Bill Norman, one of the old men from the hotel, to initiate the digging. Mom liked Bill Norman, he was quiet and didn't have an odour about him like most of the other old chaps Uncle Tommy was always bringing down to Petersfield. For three days poor Bill tried excavating the earth abutting the foundation, but the loose dry dirt just kept crumbling back to refill the hole. On the fourth day, so thoroughly frustrated, he gave up without a word and thumbed his way back home to Winnipeg.

Alex and Eddy were unlucky enough to be spending a week of their summer vacation with us during the full implementation of this great undertaking. It had rained a couple of days prior to their arrival so the earth was moist and sticky, ideal for digging. Shovels were issued to the two boys as well as Victor and Philip and lemonade was served at regular intervals. The trench would eventually be filled with the earth that the boys laboriously excavated, piling it high and thus making a bank of dangerously un-shored wet mud. Day after day the boys emerged from the grave-like hole, glistening wet and red from the relentless afternoon sun. The day the thin tar was painted on the po-rous cement, they surfaced, burned to blisters and dizzy from the fumes. They slept fitfully at night, muscles ach-ing and skin covered with layers of mint-scented creams. Many laborious hours were clocked and every evening, Memere meted out their meagre earnings. After supper most nights, we played card games and the boys, who insisted on gambling, frittered away their day's rewards on rounds of hearts and seven-up. Eddie and Alex returned to the city after a week's toil, surely wondering if it was all worth a couple of fish dinners, ten gallons of lemonade and a few stale chocolates.

When Uncle Tommy drove out to Petersfield the next spring, he found the basement, resembling an old dilapi-dated swimming pool, filled with cold spring water. Nobody told Alex and Eddy.

Now cousin Philip was a handsome boy with dark hair, brown eyes and flawless olive skin. He was the first of us cousins to try all the taboos, all the things we wanted to do but were afraid. He smoked filterless cigarettes, al-ways having one perched behind his ear or flicking from between his fingers. I'm sure he guzzled a beer or two and there were whispers of a girl somewhere, although

I never saw her. It was all a big secret; the kind teenage boys share only with their male peers. Living in the city, he sometimes ran with a rough crowd and was acquainted with both the cops and robbers. At Petersfield he could be true to himself. He could revert back to that grubby little kid he once was, playing with frogs, nuzzling little brown bunnies and throwing fearsome fits when he lost his hard earned chocolates in games of cards or a few measly pennies at rummoli. Despite his "tough-guy" façade, he was a tender soul and maybe a little too sensitive for a teenager who should be thinking only of fun things.

Victor seldom made a fuss over anything. He had his own idea of how life should be and stubbornly would not accept any deviation to his plans. He seemed to take events in stride and seldom became flustered over the unexpected. One time, he was settled in his wicker chair and fishing from the dock, when a youngster from the visiting Baggley clan, was playing on the edge, leaning over to see his reflection in the green water. The child fell in head first, hardly making a splash. Only a few bubbles rose from under the dock, as Victor calmly leaned over, reached down and pulled the boy by the scruff of his neck from the cool water. The little guy sputtered and threw up before being whisked away by his concerned parents. Victor never left his seat and said little. It was his way, always composed, except maybe once.

Victor was usually relegated to chauffeur Auntie Emma and Memere on short boat rides. One particular day, Memere decided she would like a private tour of the channel and marsh. Victor was waiting in the boat, his back to the dock, tinkering with the motor when Memere, clad in her pink flowered "touring" dress, sauntered across the dock on her squat little legs and stepped down, one foot on the dock and one in the boat. As the boat pushed away, Mom stood frozen to the porch, speechlessly watching as Memere was performing the splits over the gap, her bloomers reflecting in the still water below. Memere's best hope was Yvonne. Now Yvonne was always the slowpoke, last in everything. Not so this day. Yvonne was a blurred streak as she darted across the dock, grabbing Memere's arm for what seemed an eternity, then as if in slow motion, set her ungracefully back on the welcoming solidness of the old grey wood. Victor received a stern tongue-lashing from Auntie Emma and there were an extra couple of stale chocolates for Yvonne that evening after dinner.

Petersfield was home to many animals I considered to be exotic. There were red winged and yellow-headed black birds, skunks racoons and possum, creatures seldom encountered in the city. Once in a while, I'd spy a bobcat scampering up the road to Gilberts and of course there were cattle and turkeys living on the property that sat on the second last corner before turning towards our place. We had our own domesticated critters, little furry ones that lived in the house with us. They helped themselves to food that wasn't protected in tin containers and left tell tale signs of their presence. Auntie Emma unleashed the occasional scream as the furry brown mice showed themselves to her and she grunted in disgust when finding nibbles taken from oatmeal boxes or little brown bodies in the bottoms of empty coke bottles.

One black night as Mom, Andre and I were deep in slumber, we were simultaneously awakened by a munching sound on our side of the closed bedroom door. Mom groped around in the dark for her trusty sliver coloured flashlight Grandpa had won for her when playing bingo at Winnipeg Beach. She pointed it toward the sound and clicked the switch to reveal a small, brown field mouse sitting on the multicoloured braded rug just in front of the door. It was dwarfed by the scotch mint candy held tightly in it's little, pink paws. Mom was horrified, voicing her disgust at the fact the little rodent had obviously been rummaging through her underwear drawer, the one in which she kept her stash of hard candies. As Mom made her move, the mouse shoved the big mint in it's mouth and headed for the crack under the door. Now, mice can squeeze through the most minute of spaces, not so scotch mint candies. The little rodent's body was on one side of the door, it's sweet filled cheeks on the other. In the flurry of excitement, it finally relinquished its prize and ran for its life. Only moments passed before the whole house was awakened, everyone except Memere, gathered in our room to see what caused such a commotion. Mom recounted the mousy story to Auntie's saucer-like eyes as cousin Phil searched the house, under sofas and in closets, trying in vain to catch a glimpse of our little thief. Eventually, we all settled and climbed back into bed. Memere's room remained quiet through the episode. Auntie slept fitfully that night in the new knowledge that mice must be able to climb. Little Andre waited till we were all sleeping deeply, then quietly left his bed to set out a fresh scotch mint candy on the braided carpet near the bedroom door to replace the one lost in the skirmish.

I am told, if you see one mouse, be assured there are many more. We must have housed generations, mommies and grandmas, teens and tots. These creatures resided, happy and warm in the over-stuffed furniture of the house all winter and probably took offence when we arrived in the summer, acting as if we owned the place.

Along with the interesting creatures adding colour to our surroundings were the amusing buzzards, Uncle Tommy often brought from the hotel. Some old guys were like part of his family. In the early years, special ones were even trusted with the care of his children when he and Auntie Lil indulged in a rare night out. All the hotel lodgers were guests at the family Christmas dinner, given first cut of the succulent, stuffed turkey Auntie Lil spent hours roasting.

One of the regulars at the hotel beer parlour would say the place was the "college of knowledge." He'd arrive at the parlour opening time to see a few old fellows quietly occupying tables, staring into space or studying the pattern in the linoleum floor. After a few glasses of the honey coloured, foamy-topped elixir, they became experts, knowing everything, having been everywhere and done everything.

Oftentimes Uncle Tommy was the only one to sit by deathbeds, consoling tired old hearts and attending funerals, sometimes he and Camille being the only ones to mourn. Besides having nicknames for all of us kids, Uncle Tommy tagged most of the old-timers and friends at the hotel. They were given in good humour and most wore the monikers with pride.

In later years, long after Auntie Lil passed on, Mom would mend the wear on Uncles white shirts and navy pants. One day she mentioned he might want to dispose of one of his older shirts, as the cuffs were a little frayed. The following Sunday, when he arrived with his laundry, he casually mentioned that Cranky John had died. He was buried Friday and looked quite dapper in his red tie and a white shirt with slightly frayed cuffs. Cranky John spent many winters sleeping in dark, doorways and eating from garbage cans before being discovered by Camille one night. John was dozing under a piece of cardboard in the hotel garage. Upon being ushered inside, Uncle Tommy put him up in room number 14, on the second floor. He took to the place right away and stayed until the day he died but preferred to sleep on the hard wooden chairs lining the walls of the lobby. It wasn't that he disliked his room, he just enjoyed the open space of the lobby and mingling with others of the same cut as he. In winter, he shovelled the sidewalks in front of the hotel as well as the garage driveway and then would cross the street to make neat, the sidewalk in front of the funeral home. When eligible for old age pension cheques, he refused to take them to the bank. Instead, Camille cashed them, then kept the money behind the bar, doling it out to meet John's needs. When John died, there was $4000.00 behind the bar with his name on it. The funeral director across the street provided his services and a finely polished, wooden coffin at a deep discount price. The balance of the monies was taken to John's only relative, his sister. I'm told; she had a grand stone marker placed at the head of his grave so whoever passes knows that Cranky John lies there.

Now, Memere cared just as deeply about these old men, but wasn't noted for tolerating ignorance, which old Joe "Rosebush" found out soon enough. Late one hot dry afternoon at Petersfield, while half dozing, Memere noticed Joe pass by the window with a galvanized pail in hand and going toward the back of the house. A few minutes later, he passed by the window again heading in the same direction. After the third lap, now curious, Memere stepped out on the front porch to catch Joe on his fourth round. She inquired as to what he was doing to which he explained, Auntie Lils nasturtiums were looking a bit parched and so he was trying to locate the water tap. Memere looked at Bill, lifted her eyes to the grand, watery expanse of the creek, which was not a hundred and fifty feet in front of them and yelled, "you fool!" before returning to the open front door, leaving Joe "Rosebush" to figure it out for himself.

There was one elderly gentleman that captured young Andre's imagination. His name was Carson and Andre immediately likened him to Kit Carson following him everywhere, like a one-man posse. Outside, in the expanse of well cut lawn, lived colonies of gophers that left the area looking at times like a big muffin tin. Carson was left behind one Sunday to help dig Auntie's big garden and fill up the offending gopher holes. Little Andre spent hours with him, flushing out the vermin and filling the hollows with sand and earth, to ensure Memere's safety while mowing grass. One day, Andre was at one opening and Carson was standing by the other end. A frightened gopher leaped from the hole, scooted up inside Carson's pant leg, over the crotch and out the other leg. It made its escape, leaving Carson quite shaken with the thought of what could have been. He was immediately consoled with a warm brandy from Auntie Emma's private stock and took the rest of the day off to calm down under the shade of one of our old elms.

The Roblin hotel was demolished in 1994, while Uncle Tommy was in the hospital, recovering from a bout of ill health. He then moved into a bright little room in a nursing home overlooking the graveyard of the St. Boniface Cathedral. He died on September 14th 1996, my birthday.

Most of the old fellows who called the hotel home are gone, probably playing cards with Memere around an old table somewhere being kept honest by a couple of angels with poker faces.

I learned many things during those summers at Petersfield. I learned, young children seldom float; frightened gophers have the ability to bring a grown man to his knees and I also witnessed how far a person could stretch.

Most importantly, I learned to never take for granted a person's shortcomings, because they can sometimes be overcome in an instant.

City Boys

# IN SUSAN'S SHOES

Among the many fiends and neighbors who came to visit us during our summer holidays at Petersfield, were Susan and Buddy Jackson.

They entered our lives in the mid 1950's and soon became the focal point of many of our conversations, filling them with punctuations of laughter as well as regrets.

Our acquaintance began in the sunny summer month of June when Dad was taking a break one Saturday from his weekend chores of pretending to mow the lawn and trim the hedges. He had easily perfected the art of just looking busy and carefully groomed me to follow his lead. That day, he decided to treat my pal Linda and me to an icy cola from the gurgling chest cooler in the drug store across the street.

The shop, with its dusty shelves lined with colorful elixir bottles, cosmetics and perfumes and displays of comic books and glossy Hollywood-type magazines, was the kind of place that rests in the cobwebbed memories of so many of us. The white stucco building with expansive windows below maroon and yellow striped awnings housed a wonderful lunch counter with red-topped swivel stools and holds of sweet cold ice cream. There was strawberry ripple, French vanilla and Mom's favorite maple walnut and even my usual choice of licorice that was as black as sludge.

The sound of the milk shake machine and the smells of grilled burgers and onions lured Dad most Saturday afternoons. He would spend many hours there puffing on Black Cat cigarettes, sipping tan-colored sweet coffee and gabbing with Susan, the waitress. It was that day, when in the company of Linda and myself, he mentioned that Mom wanted to put our garage up for rent. We didn't own a car and Mom was concerned that the garage would become cluttered with Dad's abandoned hobbies. His comment presented the opportunity for us to meet Buddy, Susan's husband.

Buddy came knocking at our back door that evening right after his shift ended at the city post office. He and Mom agreed on a monthly rate, which he paid in advance, allowing him to move his Studebaker into our garage. I remember, it was blue with funny windows and it was Buddy's pride and joy. He was a mechanic by trade but had to change careers when diagnosed with a severe case of asthma. Nevertheless, he still kept that big auto humming with regular tune-ups and oil changes. It seemed, every other evening, when not on shift, he spent under that car, just his legs visible, sticking out like two sturdy little trees.

Buddy was of medium height and a bit stocky. His head was woven with black curly hair; he wore thick glasses and his barrel chest was slightly over-exaggerated. His skin was mapped with thin red threads and blotchy purple bruises, which he attributed to the effects of the steroid puffer that took prominence in the breast pocket of his colorful plaid shirts.

Buddy and Sue lived two short blocks from our house in a suffocatingly small apartment. There wasn't much room for two rather large people to stretch, so Buddy spent a great deal of time at our place. He would tinker on his car or do odd jobs around our house and yard, being under the impression that Dad's war injury hindered his ability to perform certain tasks and who was Dad to contradict his thoughts?

Buddy had a naive confidence in his own talents and always came up a bit short. There was the time he fixed one of Memere's Petersfield lawn mowers and had two pieces left over after re-assembly. Another time he excitedly trimmed the lilac hedge with Mom's new florescent orange electric trimmer. Before he was done, he snipped off the cord a couple of feet from the handle. Mom didn't care about the unfinished job, she was just thankful he hadn't electrocuted himself and the hole in the hedge grew back in no time.

Since we didn't have an automobile, Buddy and Sue took me for the occasional car ride out to Winnipeg Beach, to spend the day with his relatives. His uncle had a quaint, little cottage right on the shore. I spent many happy hours wading in the sandy-bottomed water and gambling the pennies Buddy gave me in card games with his kin.

One clear January Tuesday, when I was about eleven, Buddy thought it would be interesting to visit Petersfield in winter. He and Susan came to fetch me about ten a.m. and we headed north on the cold gray highway. Upon reaching Petersfield, we found the road plowed only to Chesley's. The stretch past our place to Cameron's was a pristine blanket of white. Buddy, being the adventurous sort, turned his blue Studebaker onto the hidden road, forgetting halfway, that the deep ditches were also hidden. It was only moments before the two right wheels of the car were stuck into the depth of the ditch. Buddy got out of the hopelessly stuck automobile, surveyed the situation and quickly devised a plan. He placed me in the driver's seat, positioned my inexperienced hands on the steering wheel, set my right foot on the gas pedal, and told me to press down firmly and steer when he yelled, "NOW". Buddy and Sue plodded through the snow and positioned themselves behind the mired vehicle. As they both dug in and pushed, Buddy yelled, "NOW" and I pressed on the pedal as mightily as I could. The car groaned into a roar, leapt from the ditch and careened down the road with Buddy in hot pursuit, yelling "BRAKE, BRAKE". Buddy had forgotten to show me the brake pedal. It seemed longer, but only seconds passed before I steered to the other side of the invisible road, taking the ditch with all four wheels. Buddy caught up, dived into the snow and opened the door to remove the keys, which killed the racing engine. I was crying, Buddy's asthmatic chest was wheezing like a pair of billows and Susan just stood in the ditch, not knowing what to do. Fortunately, a kindly farmer happened along and offered to fetch his tractor to pull us from this predicament. We didn't get to see the insilbrick house on Netley creek in winter, at least, not that day. Little was said to Mom upon our arrival home, it was our secret.

Buddy considered himself to be a protector of the vulnerable. It seemed that if anyone was experiencing difficulty, Buddy was always there to help, sometimes at risk of his own skin. One evening, he was having a bite of dinner at the local Salisbury House Restaurant when his attention was called to a couple of bullies who were badgering the young waitress. He boldly scolded them, pointed to the door and demanded their immediate departure from the diner. After he ejected the troublesome pair, he was rewarded for his bravery with a free bowl of savory stew. He also received a firm bully beating later, in the parking lot on the way to his car. Buddy's facial features were constantly changing from one disastrous adventure to the next. Stories of his daring antics were the subject of morning coffee gatherings and back fence humor.

Everyone loved Buddy; he was so good-natured and funny. He was usually the one nominated to wrench the cork from the homemade root beer, Mom brought to Petersfield. We'd all run for cover, as he'd be left trying to contain the sweet foam that billowed from the bottles. Susan, on the other hand, was as plain as Buddy was colorful. Nobody really knew Susan except maybe, Dad. He was the only one she ever really spoke with, albeit their conversations consisted of him telling stories and she giggling shyly behind cupped hands.

Buddy brought her over on occasion but usually on their way to somewhere else. She would sit quietly, her hands folded in her lap as Buddy held most of the conversation telling his amazing stories in his booming voice.

Buddy took Mom aside one time, telling her that Susan suffered with personality problems and had spent time in Selkirk Mental Hospital. It all stemmed from the abuse she had endured at the hands of her first husband. This was more than Mom wanted to know but she was content that Buddy felt comfortable enough to confide in her.

Buddy was a hero to most of the neighborhood children. He was always pulling coins from their ears and noses and treating them to ice cream from the street vendors.

Buddy was an all weather friend. He was around just as much in winter as in summer. Winter was harder on his asthma but it never stopped him from shoveling snow or helping anyone whose car needed a push. Many times his inhaler froze up and Mom would thaw it out over the warm stove element.

One day, he dropped by with Sue on their way to do some grocery shopping. They shared a pot of tea with Mom and were out the door not two minutes when Mom noticed Buddy's inhaler on the kitchen table. She ran past me to the back window, parting the curtains and peering out to the lane to see if they had left yet. She hesitated for a moment, and then turned to me, her face pale and twisted with confusion. She then told me she had just witnessed Buddy swiftly raise his hand to Susan's face, slamming her head forcefully against the top of the car seat. We stood in stiff silence, not knowing how to console each other.

Suddenly, Buddy popped his head in the back door; boisterously inquiring if anyone had seen his inhaler. Mom ran to give it to him and he was quickly gone again, this time in more ways than one. The Buddy we had known disappeared forever, replace by a stranger who could inflict physical pain on someone he professed to love. After that day, his face looked different to me. I know it didn't change, I guess it was just because of the new way I now perceived it.

One day, Susan was again admitted to Selkirk Hospital. Mother questioned Buddy as to the reason and he said he couldn't understand why the doctor accused him of being the root of Sue's problems. I think maybe, he honestly believed himself.

A few months later, a close relative of Susan's unexpectedly died and left her a considerable amount of money. It wasn't long before Buddy had Sue home again, he retired from the post office and they moved to a larger apartment downtown. We didn't see very much of them then except when they would come around to show off Buddy's new car, trailer or boat. They spent summer weekends in the little trailer, parked on Buddy's uncle's property. Buddy took up stamp collecting and used it as an excuse to come by and visit Dad. Dad had an extensive collection and they spent the odd evening pouring over albums. Sue no longer worked. She just spent her days alone in the big flavorless, apartment waiting for Buddy to come home.

It is said, just about every sad situation holds a sliver

of sunshine. And so, Buddy died at the relatively young age of 58, likely resulting from his asthma and years of inhaling strong medications. Mom tried to get in touch with Sue for two months without success as the telephone had been disconnected, indicating no alternative number and we didn't know the names of any of her relatives.

One cool, fall day a Duffy's taxi pulled up in front of our house and out stepped Susan dragging behind her a big blue Eaton's shopping bag. Mom ushered her into the house, poured her a cup of tea and inquired as to where she had been for the last two months. Sue had been very busy. She buried Buddy with all the color and ceremony afforded to the members of the Canadian Legion, then shed all that was her old life. She moved to a bright little apartment on the highway, sold Buddy's precious car, trailer and boat and bought for herself a silky black, full-length mink coat. She shared a whole pot of tea with Mom that day, laughing and talking and before she left, she presented Dad with the Eaton's shopping bag. It was carelessly stuffed with Buddy's stamp collection.

Susan lived eleven years more, cultivating new friendships, renewing old ones and continuing her loving relationship with kin. She indulged in take-out Chinese food from the Peking with my mother once a month, always arriving by taxi, wearing her shy, girlish smile and carrying a box of chocolate puffs for dessert.

She made phone calls to my Mom and me everyday, I suppose just to hear our voices as the conversations never varied. She'd tell us what she had for dinner the prior evening and giggled when we teased her about her new boyfriend. Her mantle held every card my son sent to her, extending thanks for the gifts she bestowed upon him over the years.

Susan passed away unexpectedly after taking a fall

while in the hospital for observation. She had phoned both Mom and me that night, as usual, describing to us, in great detail, what she had for supper.

I learned many things those times I spent with Buddy and Sue. It was revealed to me that there is more than one way to alter your looks and you should never allow a stupid eleven year-old to drive your car and sometimes justice is served.

Most importantly, I learned you should never wish to plant your feet in someone else's shoes because they may be far too painful to wear.

Only the names of Buddy and Susan are fictitious in this story.

# MAYBE HEAVEN IS WINNIPEG BEACH

Nana and Grandpa Sharpe were my Dad's parents. I remember Grandpa as a small man, his handsome face crowned with thick grey hair, slicked back behind his ears and a perpetual ivory smile. He seemed to have more teeth than anyone I knew.

Nana, on the other hand, was a bit plain, wore wire-rimmed glasses and seldom showed any teeth at all. Her plates spent more time soaking in a glass on her bedside table than in her mouth. She claimed they bothered her and she could eat just as well without them. Nana was quite a bit taller than Grandpa and carried considerably more weight. In contrast to her globe-shaped body, she had bird-like legs and face features. She openly adored Grandpa, he being the only person I ever saw her voluntarily embrace. She usually held her emotions deep inside, exhibiting them only by the occasional blush of her cheek or a momentary fluster in her usually calm demeanour. Grandpa hugged and kissed everyone he thought needed it, or not.

I have heard stories, which leads me to believe that they were sadly lacking in good parenting skills. When not eking out a living, they neglected my dad, in favour of relaxing with friends, liquor and a very often deck of cards.

Dad learned about life by his own experiences,

becoming mature early for his tender years. At ten, he had a paper route in the West End, up and down streets named for women, like Harriet and Isabel. "These names were quite appropriate", he'd say, "as the neighbourhood was peppered with brothels housing scarlet women." He said they were always kind to him and afforded him good tips, especially at Christmas.

He saved the meagre earnings in a glass sealer on his dresser in hopes of purchasing himself a new pair of ice skates, as almost everything he wore was hand-me-down. One day Grandpa took the money and bought Dad a second-hand pair of skates, keeping the balance for himself. Grandpa may have justified the deed in his own mind, but it would be the only story of self-pity my father would ever tell me.

Fortunately for my brother and me, God saw fit to bestow Nana and Grandpa with a forgiving son who gave them the opportunity to become wonderful grandparents.

Nana and Grandpa loved Winnipeg Beach, a small resort town, situated a few miles just north of Petersfield. They rented cabins every summer until 1959, when they purchased a wee cottage named, "Forget-me-not." It was situated on Epsilon, a quiet shady street with gravel roads, wooden sidewalks and deep ditches dotted with planks and little wooden bridges to get from the road to the slatted sidewalks.

Vacations at Winnipeg Beach were joyful times for me during the summers when I was twelve and thirteen years old, spending a few weeks alone with Nana and Grandpa and their dog, Monty. Every evening, we'd walk the three blocks to the centre of town, past an array of brightly painted cabins, across the park and down the path along the restless lakeshore, which whispered in our ears and sprinkled our faces with soft mist. Arcade music and buzzing neon lights blended fluidly on those sultry fish-fly nights as Grandpa and I couldn't wait to try our hand at manoeuvring small cranes in glass boxes for kewpie dolls and brass horse banks. We first went to the telephone building, an old two story ornate stone structure situated on a small side street across from the police station. Inside, Nana made sure I phoned home, fulfilling one of the mandatory terms of my stay. I hurriedly answered Mom's questions as Nana pumped coins into the big black phone and then we pulled away to have fun.

Nana loved to play Tango with numbered cards and hard white beans as the proprietress, Mrs. London, fussed over Grandpa. She'd squeeze his neck calling him her sweetheart and everyone would laugh with pure delight, the kind of delight that every laugh should contain. We'd indulge our cravings with vinegar on salted chips and munched on sticky red candy apples before setting out into the dark, back across the blackened park, bumping into trees and excusing ourselves.

Monty, with her sloppy kisses and wiggly behind, was always patiently waiting our return to the cozy little cabin. We seldom took her with us downtown as she had a rather strong sense of ownership, which surfaced when strangers approached. She claimed us as her own, and was especially possessive of Grandpa.

Sometimes, Nana and Grandpa stopped in at Petersfield, on the way to the Beach. Upon their arrival, Monty always escaped from the tiny car, squeezing past Nana to careen across the lawn in a blur and shoot off the end of the dock. She'd disappear in the opaque green water, under a big splash of bubbles. Everyone would hold their breath waiting for her to surface, some I'm sure, hoping she would not. Monty was not the most likeable dog, somewhat like a spoiled brat, which of course she was.

Nana and Grandpa always had dogs. The first one I re-member was a border collie-cross. His name was Mickey, and his most notable feature was the fact that he could snap a cat's neck in an instant. Then there was a nasty lit-tle terrier named Peter, who was always nipping at ankles and jumping up on my mother, tearing her nylon stockings, encouraging icy glares between Mom and Nana. Monty was a Christmas gift from Dad in 1960. He brought the whimpering little bulldog to Nana and Grandpa one cold snowy night. He came by bus, keeping the puppy warm and secure in his inside, breast pocket. Monty grew into the kind of dog only its owner could love. She was a bulky beast, white in colour with black and brown spots, baleful eyes and a knotted tail.

Mom always cringed when Grandpa offered to take us to Petersfield or Winnipeg Beach. Dad always accepted and of course, claimed the front passenger seat for himself. Mom, my little brother Andre and I would be relegated to the tiny green Austin's back seat beside Nana and Monty. The dog slobbered in the heat and closeness of the small automobile, smearing the windows and dampening Mom's lap. Monty was always used as a bad example when Mom and Dad refused Andre's pleas for a dog.

Mom has always been a bit over-protective. She felt by denying us ownership of a mutt, she was, in some way, saving us from the pain of prematurely having to deal with death. Unfortunately, she was unable to shield me from the heartbreak of losing my precious Grandpa. Nana and I mourned together, albeit, she never exhibited any tears. It was not her way. I have always been the emotional one in the family, blubbering easily even when happy.

In an effort to ease our feelings of loss, Dad arranged to send Nana and me on a weekend train ride to Grand Forks, N.D.. It turned out to be the tour of the two buffoons.

We were all thumbs, mentally as well as physically, kind of when you are trying to think of something other than what is really on your mind. Nana unknowingly caught the hem of her dress while snapping her suitcase shut when the customs officer was finished with his inspection. She was distracted with the fact that he had mistaken her for a Scotsman rather than Irish and tore away a sizeable strip of material from the skirt of her dress while rising to exit our compartment. We laughed so hard, there were tears in our eyes or maybe they were tears of guilt for feeling happy again.

I managed to spill the entire contents of my cosmetic bag, sending a multitude of shiny, cylindrical objects rolling down the centre aisle of the dining car. The train was brimming with airmen from the Grand Forks base, who immediately volunteered to help retrieve my miscellaneous bits of make-up. It was a thrill to have so many men at my feet at one time, even though it was over in minutes.

While in Grand Forks, we stayed at the Dakota hotel, the one Nana and Grandpa always checked into when visiting the States on shopping sprees. Nana loved to try new restaurants, but was always forgetting to wear her false teeth. With her funny little bird mouth, I could never tell if she had them in or not. I was taught to always be polite, so I never asked before leaving the hotel for meals. By the end of the weekend I was getting used to sprinting back to the Dakota to fetch her plate and smuggling it to her under the table.

No one ever knew if the get-away did her any good, as she never admitted to having a problem in the first place. Nana had been left alone before. After immigrating with Grandpa in 1912, he went to war. Once again in 1941, she waved good-bye to her husband and only child. Grandpa was sent to British Columbia to guard P.O.W. camps and

Dad travelled overseas, to participate in the struggle for Europe. She then had to deal with the uncertainty of Dad's being temporarily lost in action somewhere in the merciless streets of war-torn Sicily. Despite the offered support of friends, alone in her little house on Kate Street, she dealt with her plight, solitary in her façade of stone.

After the war, She and Grandpa moved to 287 Kensington Street in "sunny" St. James. Nana would never admit to the fact that it did, sometimes, rain in St. James. They settled into a green trimmed, one bedroom dwelling with flowering pink peony bushes in the front yard and a shed in the back to house Grandpa's collection of everything he ever owned. Setting off the front of the little bungalow was a cosy screened-in porch, over-stuffed with a mildewed, old Toronto couch, two sinkingly-soft arm chairs, a jungle of plants grown wild and several embroidered cushions depicting bull dogs and the Union Jack.

Grandpa raised budgie birds in the porch during summer, relocating the cages of little blue and green birds to the bedroom in winter. I would love to lie on their bed after Christmas dinners, deep among the cool darkness and coats listening to the little budgies muttering to each other.

Alone once again, Nana eventually managed to get her life in order and soldier on through her time of adjustment. Unfortunately, Monty had a much more difficult time. She guarded all that was Grandpa's, especially his old armchair, the one with the big cross-stitched pillowed seat. The poor thing was so consumed with grief; she seldom ate and could no longer cope. Nana had to call for help one cold rainy day, when she found Monty in the back yard, angry and viciously inconsolable.

Before winter set in that year, Nana sold her little one bedroom house on Kensington Street and moved to a high-rise just two streets over. From that day on she never really spent much time in the city, at least not mentally. The long cold winters, cooped up in her sparse apartment, afforded her dreams of the beach. She went through the motions of living every day, warming TV dinners, playing Bingo at the Blue Bird Club on Wednesday nights and generally putting in time till she was once again on highway #9, headed north.

I used to wonder why she looked so forward to a summer of fetching water in galvanized pails from the corner of the street and "spending a penny" as she called it, in the decrepit old outhouse. Mom found the tumbled down little two-seater smelly and disgusting, so for Nana's birthday one year, she had a nice new one delivered from a local carpenter's shop. It was painted green, the same shade as the one we used in Petersfield. I guess the colour was thought to blend into the surrounding foliage. I considered Nana's facility just as smelly and spider infested as the one at Petersfield. She always installed a freshener, which looked like a block of icy snow, but smelled like mothballs. It only served to blend with the residing odour that permeated the place, making the air doubly insulting to my nose. A man with a horse-drawn wagon came once a week, usually in the night to empty the pail from behind a flap in the back of the outhouse. Nana was caught once with her "pants down" so to speak. It was earlier in the evening when the "honey wagon" came this once. Nana was inside, at the time, having to deal with the clamour and intrusion of her privacy as Mom and Dad snickered silently to each other in the yard, waiting to see the outcome. When the wagon finally moved on, Nana emerged with an unassuming look on her face. She knew of course, even if she had threatened Dad to hold his tongue, it would have been useless. He was only too pleased to tease her mercilessly and recounted the episode to willing ears for years to come.

There was some concern about Nana's safety, as she grew older, still insisting on spending her summers at the beach. Dad went down by bus most weekends. Everyone commented on what a wonderfully unselfish son he was. Our thoughts were likewise until we realize the bus was air-conditioned, Nana cooked only what she believed to be his favourite meals and he wiled the hours away, undisturbed, sleeping in the shady screened-in porch. Even on cool rainy days, that porch was a wonderful escape. With the screened front open to nature, one could smell the cedars and pines permeating the moist air with their perfumes. Enchanting whistles and songs from colourful birds, bobbing in the leafy ceiling above the small white and green cottage, filled the porch with a feeling of being unencumbered from the worries and humdrum of city life.

One particularly warm summer after Nana recovered from a massive heart attack, Mom decided to have a phone installed in the main room of the small cottage, for our sake as much for Nana's. Nana considered the intrusion of her privacy unnecessary until one, dark, night when she fell out of bed. The old bedside table broke her fall but also opened a sizable gash across her forehead. She lay on the floor for a very long fifteen minutes, recovering from shock and vocally reprimanding herself for being so clumsy. Then, realizing blood was trickling down her face into her eyes, she composed herself and dialled the R.C.M. Police. They immediately had an ambulance dispatched from Gimli Hospital, just a few miles north on highway #9. If the paramedics were having a bad night then, it would only get worse. Upon their arrival, they were greeted by this gritty old woman, who would hear nothing of going to the hospital. She had already decided she would not lie on a stretcher in the back of any ambulance. They finally convinced Nana to join them in the front seat of the vehicle,

135

she, sitting in the middle with one of the attendants holding a compress to her forehead as they sped down the road to Gimli. With sirens wailing and lights flashing, they arrived at the emergency ward. The doctor on call set seven stitches in her forehead, then she, still in her night attire, managed to procure a ride back to Winnipeg Beach with the Gimli town taxi.

In 1970, my brother Andre was about twenty years old and employed as a lineman with the provincial hydro company. He spent a viciously cold winter de-icing electrical lines which hung from pole to pole down icy Manitoba highways and back country roads. He was relieved when the winter sun warmed into spring and then to summer. A new assignment put his way, was the construction of a small sub-station on highway #9 between Petersfield and Winnipeg Beach. Nana was more than pleased to have Andre living in the little cottage with her. She tried her best to serve nutritious meals, cooked on the sooty, old wood stove and packed lunches in brown paper bags for him every day. Now, Nana wasn't noted for her culinary skills. She could make a killer steak and kidney pie and her Yorkshire pudding was superb, but that was about it. By the end of six weeks, Andre's stomach became queasy at just the thought of fish stick dinners and lobster pate sandwiches. He lied, telling Nana the job was done, waved good-bye and moved down the road into the quiet, six-bedroom insilbrick house on Netley Creek. Andre finished out the summer scaling the beams and pilings of the substation, sleeping late on weekends and playing poker with the guys.

Directly across the street from "Forget-me-not" sat the "Ramona," an equally small cottage. Appropriately, it was owned by a family of very small people, not one of them being over five feet. Longevity was a family endowment; Mr. Dunach and his wife were each just a couple of years short of hundred. Nana and I spent one weekend making pastel coloured Kleenex flowers to decorate the "Ramona" for the Dunach's seventy-fifth wedding anniversary party. I have not since met anyone having been married that many years. The fete was a boisterous affair, well attended by friends and beach neighbours. There was a ruby coloured punch and dainty sandwiches along with a bottomless chilli pot. A horseshoe tournament was held on the pitch in the side yard. Horseshoe tournaments took place in the side yard most weekends, not just for special occasions. It would have been unusual for Saturday and Sunday to go by without the sound of shoes clinking on iron spikes and oohs and aahs wafting through the neighbourhood. The Dunach family was small in numbers, as well as stature.

Besides the old people, there were two daughters, one son-in-law and one grandson. The son-in-law drove a big old Eatons delivery truck. He had removed the name from the side of the vehicle, but it was still painted the familiar red and navy blue. The interior resembled someone's living room, furnished with two cushy sofas and an easy chair. Most warm, summer evenings the truck would be parked on Main street, the nose to the curb and back doors open to the street. It was filled with small people, laughing and eating French fries and corn on the cob from chip stands on the Boardwalk. This little gathering usually included one large woman, with bird legs, eating an ear of golden buttered corn on a stick. On those nights she always remembered to bring along her teeth. If she caught sight of me, she'd call out "woo-hoo" in that funny little voice of hers, then quickly return to the conversation within the truck.

As Nana's age began to show, so too did that of the little green and white cottage. Dad could manage to slap on a lick of paint on weekends and later, Andre was recruited to make repairs here and there. Grandpa knew what chores had to be done on a regular basis, but he left us so suddenly; no one thought to ask him.

One chilly August evening, when I was about nineteen, we learned just how important upkeep was. Nana and I decided to take a walk downtown as there was a James Bond movie playing at the little theatre on the end of the boardwalk and Nana suggested she might like to see it. She set a fire in the wood stove, expecting the cabin to be toasty warm for our arrival home. We made the 8 p.m. show, indulged in boxes of stale salty popcorn and at 10 p.m., set off along the dark streets home. We cut through the park, bumping into trees and excusing ourselves. Nana then pulled out one of those silver flashlights Grandpa won in a Boardwalk game. Flashlights were a necessity as street lamps were sparse, sitting atop only corner poles, leaving the middle of the blocks really black. The faint glimmers of cottage windows were visible but the light was never strong enough to reach the sidewalks. When we neared home, Nana commented on the unusual number of fireflies flitting about over her cottage. As we came closer, we realized they were clearly not fireflies. Sparks were shooting from the chimney into the dark night, settling dangerously on the roof, nestling in the trees and floating gently to the ground. We unlocked the door and rushed into the kitchen, which was aglow from the bright orange stovepipe. Nana grabbed the poker, pulling the round, element lid open as I poured in a bucket of rainwater. A great sizzle erupted; spewing steam and flash into the kitchen, settling to paint a grey film over everything. We then, gingerly tapped the pipe with the poker, loosening the burning creosote, clearing the plugged vessel as glowing chunks dropped into the wet mess in the bottom of the stove. Totally exhausted, we left the clean up for morning and crawled into our beds, leaving the fate of our "counterfeit" fireflies in the hands of our guardian angels.

Nana went on to spend every summer at the beach until her unexpected passing during the 1974 Christmas season. She was 81 years old. We found her in her bed, her face serene and eyes closed in boundless sleep. I'm sure her soul flew by Winnipeg Beach for one last look before moving on to meet Grandpa or maybe, he was there, waiting for her on the boardwalk.

In the spring of 1975, Dad had the little cottage bull-dozed. His mind held thoughts of a modern place, a place he could spend his idle time in retirement years. Unfortunately, red tape and zoning laws prohibited his dreams to become reality and the little lot was left to support nothing but weeds for the next three decades.

I learned many important things, those summers with Nana. I learned outhouses all smell the same, to never to argue with an old person and fireflies are not usually orange.

Most importantly, I learned there is no easy way to deal with death. We just have to believe our loved ones are waiting to meet us in heaven, or at least wherever we wish heaven to be.

Nana, Grandpa and Monty
Dad and little Alec

# THE RUBE

Our dear Alma was one of Auntie Emma's closest friends. She owned and worked a big garden plot on highway #9. Her stubby "green" fingers and strong wide back transformed the barren soil each spring into a couple dozen rows of tall swishing corn stalks, ripe with ears of golden bantam and mounded trails of bushy, green potato plants. Bulging, misshapen beefsteak tomatoes were her passion, growing on monstrous bushes, to obscene sizes and plentiful enough to supply all her friends and family. She had only a few miles further to come to see us when we vacationed at Petersfield. Alma often arrived with her car brimming with fresh carrots, homemade dill pickles, perogies and holobchi marinated in chunky tomato sauce. Weekday visits seemed to be her favorite times. I think she preferred the concentrated attention afforded her when she was the only guest, avoiding the Saturdays and Sundays, which were polluted with the noise that comes with crowds.

Our old insilbrick house welcomed many friends looking for escape from the summer city heat. Games of baseball and golf in the large freshly mown backyard were on-going, we children vying to beat each other in the tournaments Dad enthusiastically arranged to keep us busy and out of mischief. Most of the adults found relief in the shady screened porch and clinking glasses of lemon gin, while others busied themselves nibbling through my Aunties' plentiful gardens and indulging in sweet yellow plums under the leafy umbrella of thorny orchard trees.

Alma was a tall, solid woman of "good Ukrainian stock". She was as hard working as any big, muscular man and yet endeavored to exhibit the gentility of a delicate southern belle, often speaking though pursed lips and sipping tea with an extended pinky finger. Her garden attire consisted of dusty coveralls and a white scarf wrapped around the back of her head and knotted in front, 1920's style. When socializing, she usually wore one of her many flowered shirtwaist dresses with matching shoes and noisy, chunky jewelry. Her mousy brown hair, always salon-fresh was piled in sausage curls on top of her head and her face, perfectly tinted with the latest shades in lipstick, rouge and eye shadow. Her oversized purses jingled and clinked with frosted, glass jars of moisture cream, perfume atomizers and at least a couple of crimson lipsticks with matching bottles of nail polish. She was surely Auntie's best Avon customer, spending many afternoons drinking coffee and plucking her choices from the cosmetic delights crammed into and atop Auntie's dining room buffet.

Alma's cavernous, stately home in Winnipeg's north end occupied a huge, grassy yard in the prestigious area along the Red River. The streets there were lined with towering ancestral trees shading expansive lawns and aromatic flower gardens. Her home was meticulously neat, filled with elegant antique furniture and pricey knick-knacks contradicted by shining, crinkle-skinned rings of home-made garlic sausage hanging to dry in the sparkling glassy sunroom.

It was really hard to stick to my diet when spending time with Alma. Her idea of a light snack was her special deep-fried chicken in crispy, golden beer batter or a good helping of potato and green onion perogies served piping hot with a side of cold sour cream.

Alma was a born matchmaker, always winking and poking at me when she noticed what she decided was a handsome catch. I would shudder if Alma arrived unannounced at Petersfield when Victor and Philip's friends were there. Their presence just supplied more fuel for her suggestive little hints, sending Yvonne, Linda and me to find places of seclusion to cool our red faces. The embarrassment never lasted long as our more composed faces could always be counted around the table come suppertime.

Alma loved the countryside in summer and would take Auntie Emma, Yvonne and me for car rides on sunny, warm days. She'd roll down the windows of her great, roomy Mercury; turn up the radio and head out to the highway. Singing some of her favorite Elvis tunes, she'd wave randomly to people on the streets, proving there was not a thread of embarrassment in her fiber. If she happened to eye what she considered to be potential boyfriend material in a passing car or motorcycle, she'd wolf-whistle and point invitingly to poor Yvonne and me, as we sank cringing in the back seat.

Alma introduced me to her son Jack when I was eighteen. In contrast to his mother, he was small-boned, fair and fine featured. He wore small, wire-rimmed glasses and the top of his head was hidden under loosely curled, golden hair. He conversed with a most wry sense of humor and was five years older than I. Alma was delighted when we found interest in each other, as she had been extolling his attributes to me for months. She had dreams of a big wedding accommodating a "pay sucker" band, a full Ukrainian dinner of turkey, meatballs in rich brown gravy, the traditional holobchis and a rousing presentation with the groom being turned upside down by his best man and the bride paraded around on the shoulders of some gentlemen guests and ushers. But most importantly, Alma ached to become a grandmother.

Jack and I dated for a while, taking in the odd movie or football night game at Winnipeg Stadium, watching a bunch of men in tights and large shoulders menacingly facing each other before clashes and cracking sounds of helmets on helmets piercing the steady hum of die-hard fans. My favorite times were evenings spent dining on jumbo shrimps, sipping red house wine and slow dancing with Jack in the filmy romantic light of Chan's Moon Room.

Before the spring of 1963, Jack left to accept an engineering job in Northern Quebec. We wrote and sent photos but our correspondence abruptly ended when he met someone else. He fell in love, delighting Alma when he brought home his bride-to-be. A flurry of socials ensued as well as bridal showers and gentlemen's stags before Alma could finally relax and look forward to the grandchildren she so desired.

Nick and Alma were the first to bring Ukrainian culture to my life. Our neighborhood was predominantly British with a sprinkling of French and people who had changed their names, in those subtly discriminatory times, to fit more securely into business and social circles.

In the 1950's and 60's, social groups, nationalities and religions were segregated in Winnipeg by hardly visible yet sturdy barriers. Certain groups of peoples, as taught by their parents, tried to impart this tradition to their own children. On the whole, I believe they failed. They made the fortunate mistake of raising pampered kids who grew into spoiled teenagers with independent minds. My pal Linda and I were Roman Catholics, taught by the nuns and priests to believe Catholics were the only people with the key to heaven. Mom was tutored in the same manner, while encased in cotton by the nuns of a French convent during her formative years, yet had difficulty clinging to all of the set rules. Mom and Dad's house was open to everyone, no matter what creed or race, just so long as they didn't want to date their daughter.

Linda and I enjoyed more lax curfews than our parents and were offered higher educations. Television widened our eyes to the world, stretching us to touch other cultures, races and religions. We were made sorely aware of the injustices acquainted with racism and war and encouraged to raise our voices in protest. Much to our parents' dismay, we did make waves in our own little spaces.

One fresh sunny Petersfield afternoon, Linda and I were lazing on the dock feeling quite bored. We heard the roar of a powerful motor rounding the point at Gilberts resort and onto the creek. We took interest, as it was unusual to see strangers on the water in the middle of the week. The craft was one of those new fancy fiberglass speedboats that just skimmed the water, leaving a foaming wake behind it. As the boat neared, Linda and I perked up, realizing the passengers were two handsome young men. We both decided, in a spit moment, to be daring. We waved to the boys, and much to our surprise, they steered the boat toward our dock. We weren't sure whether to run or smile. We smiled. They pulled up side, obviously determined to make our acquaintances using stutter-punctuated pick-up lines and nervous grins.

Auntie Emma appeared, as if out of nowhere, carrying a tray upon which was centered a glass jug of pale lemonade jammed with clinking ice-cubes. She offered us four glasses and a plate of maple flavored sandwich cookies, Memere's favorites. Her demeanor was uncharacteristically over-pleasant and her face noticeably strained with a puckered smile. She then quickly returned to the house to join Mom and Memere peering through the curtained living-room window.

A seven o'clock date was made to meet the boys at Chesley's for a cola and maybe, a plate of fries. As with most things, we made the date without asking permission first. Surprising to us, permission was denied, the reason being the color of their skin and the slant of their eyes. Not unlike most strong-willed fourteen year-olds, we rebelled, crying and screaming and around seven that evening, we sneaked out the back door and down the gravel road to Chesley's. The boys weren't there. We were stood up. I felt hurt and disappointed that I had gotten into all of this trouble for nothing. I wondered what could have happened. Maybe the boys had led us on or maybe their parents didn't want them to go out with us.

One of Victor and Philip's many close friends was a chubby, freckle-faced Jewish boy with a silver front tooth. His given name was Earl, but everyone called him "The Rube". He spoke with a Groucho Marx accent, wore his trouser belt high above his waist and tried his best to aggravate me every chance he was given. The Rube and I didn't get along, ever criticizing each other's dominant physical features. His freckles and mean disposition became the focus of my needling, as he was persistent in pointing out my adolescent plumpness. He called me "chickie", in fact he called all the girls "chickie". He called my mother and Auntie, "Mrs. Chickie". He didn't have a name for Memere. He didn't dare.

One crystal clear morning, the sunshine was bouncing off the ripples on the creek. It was promising to be a hot day as the old dock was already starting to sizzle a bit. Phil, Vic and The Rube set off in the motor boat for a day of fishing, with a packed lunch, plenty of cold lemonade and a big tin can full of muddy pink worms from Auntie Emma's garden.

147

They were determined to return with their limit, no matter if they had to wile the whole day away anchored in the lush marsh or down one of the numerous channel inlets. They discovered what they thought to be the perfect spot, dropped the cinder-block-on-a-rope, which anchored the boat from meandering off on its own, and settle in for success.

The lunch was pretty well eaten by noon and the lemonade gone warm. Phil had worn a bulky-knit woolen sweater and was starting to experience intense heat with-in as the afternoon approached. He decided it would be stupid to remove the sweater and expose his yet white winter skin to the harsh, blazing sun. While pondering this dilemma with his teenaged mind, he decided it would be a good idea to just scoop cool water from the creek and douse himself with it, sweater and all. Fair-skinned, freckle-faced Earl thought this to be a wonderful idea and sprinkled himself as well, lowering his body temperature by soaking his Conway Twitty t-shirt to transparency.

The Rube idolized Conway Twitty. He knew the title of every Conway Twitty song, how many minutes it ran and the date of release. He was a walking book of information, from Conway's birthday to the brand of cream he combed through his slick black hair.

As the morning turned into afternoon, the cool water became trapped in the sweater and t-shirt, warming up and eventually boiling the contents within. All this was transpiring while Victor, who was older and wiser, lay snoozing in the bow of the boat under his big shady sombrero, his line hanging limp in the still reflection of the water.

Vic never said much at any time. It was as if he enjoyed watching the rest of us struggle and make complete fools of ourselves. He then kept reminding us of our stupidity for the rest of the holiday.

Sometime in the late afternoon, the three boys pulled

up to our dock, their limit caught, but without the usual jubilation that accompanied such a feat. Auntie noticed how especially red Phil's and The Rube's faces were. When Phil removed the sweater, we could see his back was covered with bubbled, angry blisters. A rush of activity ensued as Mom and Auntie Emma hurried to their respective bedrooms to fetch the great medicine chest and cosmetic case boasting remedies of medicated creams and salves. Phil went to bed that evening looking like strawberry cream cake, all red, white and gooey. The Rube declined the application of lotion, claiming his tender skin was superior and would, no doubt heal itself overnight.

Phil was looking much better in the morning, the blisters flattened to a soft pink. Not so, poor Earl. His blisters broke during the night while he was sleeping. The yellowish, sticky fluid dried, but at the same time, served as glue between his skin and the dirty old Conway Twitty t-shirt. He tried everything to delicately remove the shirt, from a slow peel to resoaking it, then resolved to keep it on, saving himself from a great deal of pain.

Later that day, I found my opportunity to get even for all those nasty little barbs and "chickie" remarks The Rube had been tossing my way all week. Supper was at five, the usual time and Auntie had outdone herself again. She served fried chicken, mashed potatoes with gravy, savory sage stuffing and a shredded cabbage, jellied salad with olives. The Rube was thrilled with the fare presented and loaded his plate to overflowing. As he shuffled by, his meal in hand, I whacked him on the back with all the might within me. He collapsed to his knees on the floor in a puddle of pain as everyone looked at me in horror. The satisfaction I thought I would feel disappeared in an instant and remorse invaded my soul just as quickly as the gravy and cranberry sauce soaked into the porous old hardwood floor. I also had a sinking feeling that The Rube would surely seek revenge.

It had been a long day and no one complained about having to go to bed early. Everyone was body and mind weary. Linda, Yvonne and I fell asleep quickly, Yvonne in the middle, Linda by the wall and I, as usual on the outside edge of the squeaky old iron bed. With the fresh country air in our lungs, and the warm sunny days behind us, we always slept hard and deep.

In the black quiet of that night, The Rube decided to collect his due. He emptied the pellets from his Daisey b.b. rifle and silently padded into our bedroom. Placing the gun to my head, he pulled the trigger. Almost instantly, the whole house awoke. The initial report, followed by our screams brought lights to life and footfalls rising on the stairs from the main floor. Mom and Auntie were now completely devoid of any patience they may have thought they had. Highlighting their reddened faces, were gust of uttered anger pushing through tightened lips and clenched teeth for us to return to our beds, turn off the lights out and go to back to sleep. As if we could. I tossed and turned, my mind abuzz with what I might do to sooth my wounded pride. Nothing brilliant came to mind, as Linda, Yvonne and I tried to plot and plan; we were just too tired to fuss about it and eventually dropped off to sleep.

The next morning, Alma came by in her big, two-toned olive green Mercury. She brought a big batch of fried chicken and a few dozen perogies. We spent that day indulging in the fattening treats and laughing at Alma's jokes. It was always good when company came, as we were not expected to work when guests were with us.

When Alma left for the city that evening, she had an unexpected passenger, in the form of a chubby, freckled fifteen year-old with a silver front tooth and wearing a soiled Conway Twitty t-shirt.

I learned many things during those summers at Petersfield. I learned home-made garlic sausage can live harmoniously in the same house with expensive antique furniture, cool water mixed with warm sunshine can make red lobsters out of little shrimps and a big two-toned, olive green car is not an attractive sight.

Most importantly, I learned that revenge never accomplishes anything. At best, it may just fill your heart with shame or buy you an unexpected ride home.

A summer of best friends
Linda, Yvonne, the boys and me

# IMAGINE

$I$t was hard to imagine on a warm breathless Petersfield
night, any other season but summer could be there. My
mind never imagined the green lush orchard, Auntie's abundant garden and the sizzling second floor of that creaky old
house could ever be cold and covered in snow.

Pepere Roy's business was seasonal, only entertaining
hunters and fishermen in the summer and fall. He never
spent a winter at Petersfield.

Thinking he might the year he moved in, provisions
were brought in for the short cold days and long frozen
nights. A large pile of chopped wood sat just across from
the side door, against the fence of crooked gray saplings
he shared with his neighbor and a six months supply of
jugged, artesian well water settled at the bottom of the
basement stairs. Since there was no running water in the
house and the creek would be frozen, he procured a large
tub for melting snow and an oversized aluminum kettle to
warm the water over the woodstove fire. If nothing else, he
figured to be warm and clean.

The hungry furnace in the cold damp basement consumed many pieces of split poplar and oak as the ground
froze to cement and frost sucked the green from the trees
and summer vegetation. Brown bulrushes popped in the
cold north wind and the creek murmured softly under a

thin layer of ice and dusty snow. Billows of heat rushed through the registers to the main floor of the damp old house, but failed to dry the timbers and left cold the areas around the doors, which spread and crept across the hardwood floors. Pepere soon fell ill with chills, weakened limbs and shortness of breath forcing him to send word to Winnipeg, asking Uncle Tommy for his help.

Uncle and his friend Jack drove out on the bleak, winter highway but could only get as far as Trossi's turkey farm. Across a blanketed white field they could see Pepere's lonely looking insilbrick structure on the banks of the now solidly frozen creek. Uncle Tommy hired a cutter, fashioned from shiny black iron and harnessed to a couple of hefty, wooly-footed horses to navigate the short journey. The snow was beaten hard from the merciless prairie winds enabling the horses to gallop across the field with relative ease, pushing great gusts of steam from their huge winking nostrils. The wire fencing was banked in high drifts, which were scaled by the hardy beasts with little effort. Upon arrival, Uncle Tommy bundled Pepere in a thick woolen wrap and set him on the small, thinly cushioned seat, locked the door to the house and set back into the frosty afternoon. They soon returned to the turkey farm and Jack, who had kept automobile running for warmth.

Pepere was never much of a city boy, but he was surely gad to see the bright lights and bustling streets of Winnipeg that day. He spent about a month in the St. Boniface Hospital recuperating from an especially nasty case of pneumonia and then went to live with his sister in her big three-story house on Young Street. In the following years, at the fist hint of snow, Pepere packed his little bag and moved to Winnipeg, California or wherever his whim and charming ways would take him.

Pepere was seventy-two years old at the time. Age can

often dictate to a person. At eighteen, I was fearless and certain no Petersfield winter could deter me from venturing out to have some fun. Not spending summers with Memere any longer, I sometimes traveled to Petersfield for weekends or any holiday from work that suited my friends, be they days in summer or winter.

After graduation, I attended Business College to please Dad. I really had no direction of my own, so I followed his. He attended Angus College after the war and was content working in the field of numbers. With my diploma in hand, I was hired to work in the Toll Billing department of the telephone system, spending my days installed in front of a battleship gray, metal wall of pigeonholes. The four years spent working there were an introduction to the real world. About twenty or thirty women of all ages worked in toll billing, under the management of one very handsome blue-eyed, prematurely gray-haired man who was openly having an affair with my fiery, redheaded supervisor. A wiry little woman of about sixty years occupied the desk adjacent to mine, complaining the day away through clouds of pungent smoke from the ever-present cigarettes, which discolored her bushy gray mustache. She claimed to have once spent time in the navy, which never came into dispute, as her colorful language was not unlike that of an old tar. I so often wondered where the nuns who educated me through high-school and the prissy, commercial teachers at Angus got their ideas of how one should conduct themselves while making a living in the business world. Everyone called each other by first names, regardless of maturity except, of course, that angel-eyed manager and only to his face.

One of the most outstanding women in Toll Billing was Joan. Our office was only a place she put in time, taking calls from would-be suitors and arranging her social calendar.

Her shiny auburn mane served to deepen her green eyes, which always emanated genuine interest in whom ever was in her company. She possessed an infectious, little laugh and would wink shamelessly, leaving most men noticeably shaken. While many men pursued her, Joan's love was reserved for Russell, a handsomely shy fellow who was hopelessly in love with her.

Joan reveled in the outdoors and decided, one crispy March day in 1963, to take us for a ride to Petersfield. She invited her cousin Barry, a soldier in the Princess Pats light infantry and his diminutive friend Skip, along with Russell and me to venture out on the highway in the 1951 two-toned green Buick she shared with her brother. As we approached Chesley's, we saw the road to the old insilbrick house was as smooth and white as a blank canvas, silently awaiting the color of spring. Leaving the car in Chelsey's lot, we pulled our collars to cover our ears and gingerly placing one foot in front of the other, crept atop the crusty, hard-packed snow. Then, like so many frightened gophers, we quickly dropped one by one through the deceiving cover of snow into a cold watery ditch below.

With boots filled with brown, icy-cold water, we slogged our way to the house, which welcomed us with floor-creaking frostiness. Thankfully there was a supply of dry wood in the basement and before long, the old kitchen stove was crackling with heat, its yawning oven door open to warming five pairs of solidly numbed feet. Despite damp socks and frozen toes, we endeavored to salvage the day by lifting the rings from the surface of the stove to roast marshmallows over the roaring fire and we cranked Auntie Emma's little transistor to about as loud as it could muster, dancing to keep warm. Steaming coffee was coerced from the few grains left in a tin in the otherwise empty cupboard above the open refrigerator. Time passed quickly as it always does with youthful fun and so we donned our jackets, mitts and boots in the damp moist air of the house and set out into the winter winds, sure to tread more carefully than before.

We made good time back to the car but our elation was soon dashed with the discovery that a ball bearing had somehow fallen out of the gear selector in the car, preventing Joan from shifting into first gear. The boys pushed the car and once it was in motion, she didn't dare stop. This was not a problem on the highway but the city streets required a bit of strategy, dealing with heavier traffic and synchronizing lights. As Joan maneuvered cautiously down Main Street, Barry mentioned something about having to be back in army barracks by seven. It was important that he catch the 6 p.m. bus at Mountain Avenue and Main. As we approached Mountain, Joan slowed; Barry opened the passenger side door and set his feet to the pavement. He ran alongside the car, clinging to the door as we approached the bus stop. Suddenly without a word he let go, somersaulting toward a startled, raggedly dressed, old gentleman who was waiting for the bus. As we continued down the street, we looked back to see Barry nonchalantly dusting himself off as the North Main bus was nearing the corner.

Joan managed to get the rest of us to her place without further incident and Russ drove me home, insuring a good nights sleep before work the next morning.

My position at the telephone system was very elementary. I spent boring days sorting long distant bills with six other girls, coloring our tedious hours with the gossip that a congregation of females usually finds entertaining. Young men from the data processing department situated in the basement of the square, cement colored building were always finding excuses to visit our floor, as it had the reputation of being abundant with single women. As with most offices, most of the young people spent time together after hours, some of us cultivating enduring friendships. Hours were spent smoking cigarettes, drinking far too many Rusty Nails at the Paddock cocktail lounge across the avenue and trying to find unique ways to celebrate each of our birthdays, the last being quite taxing on our imaginations.

In January 1963, we were faced with devising a new way to celebrate Irene's twenty-first. The suggestion of a party at Petersfield was tossed around and we all agreed it would be a wonderful stage for Irene's graduation to legal drinking age. The date was set, invitations were delivered by word of mouth and a big decorated, cake was ordered from the Dominion Store in the mall across the street.

I had just begun dating a fellow named, Hatch. He carried a six-foot-four frame, was very athletic and loved to dance. He envisioned himself to be another Fred Astaire. I was totally smitten with his intense passion for love and living, savoring all that was pleasing to his senses. We met in the early mornings, traveling to work on the Portage Avenue bus, holding hands till he had to depart at the Wall Street stop. Friday evenings, we attended ladies night at the races and Saturdays, we exhibited our prowess on the dance floor at weddings or socials or just sipped wine with friends in the Constellation Room at the Airport Hotel. We spoke for hours on the phone, falling asleep with each other's words in our ears.

Hatch and I drove out to Petersfield early Saturday afternoon in his 1956, blue and white Plymouth. Phoning ahead, I had asked for the road to our place to be plowed and so it was. We had to park on the road as the driveway to the house was untouched. The expanse of the yard was covered in brilliant crusty white, clumps of snow hanging from the bare limbs of the orchard trees and the creek was speechless under a thick layer of gray ice. There was little sign of the life that teemed in summer. At the end of each summer, the doors to the old house were simply closed and locked as we all left for the city. No shutters were nailed over the windows or padlocks installed to protect the place from reckless winter winds or prying hands and it stood, always intact upon our arrival.

The air was clean and cold, prickling our faces to pink as we trudged to the house, which looked so familiar and yet stark against the bleak panorama. Buzzing sounds oozed from electricity pulsing through the single hydro wire above our heads as our footsteps crunched up the porch steps, across the painted wooden floor to the big brass lock on the door. With a yawning creak, the vacant house was open to us, cold and strange, but it wasn't long before Hatch set fire in the furnace and the rafters began to crackle and thump from the melting frost within. Others started arriving with cases of beer and brown bags stuffed with garlic sausage, bricks of cheese and potato chips. They came barging fearlessly through the knee-deep drifts in search of promised fun. The sun settled early, painting the snow pink momentarily and then blue under a cloak of moonlight. The house became alive in minutes, once more filled with music, food and laughter.

Irene was thrilled, making sure everyone knew as she announced her happiness with a vodka martini induced dance on the kitchen table. The party carried on for a couple of hours, glasses clinking and candles lit, beer spilled on hardwood floors and the gooey cake gobbled to nothing but a few sweet crumbs. Larry, from Data Processing brought Steve, an old flame of mine to the party. I was surprised to see his ruddy, acned face as he sauntered by with a party hat clinging to his head. He said something about having a great time as he planted a kiss on my lips and took a seat in the corner, in Memere's old wicker chair. I proceeded to the kitchen to check on the food only seconds before hearing a kafuffle break out in the living room. It lasted a second or two and when it was over, the tri-light lampshade was as crumpled as Steve's nose. That was the moment I found out just how passionate Hatch really was.

As with some distasteful things, the incident did have a fortunate side. When Steve was leaving prematurely, he discovered Irene, the birthday girl, passed out and sitting in a pile of snow just beside the porch. Her pants were around her ankles; she hadn't been able to find our little green outhouse despite the brilliant moonlight. Irene would spend the next month suffering the consequences, perched on a donut cushion in front of her keypunch machine.

After the last headlights disappeared in the then dark Petersfield night, Hatch and I gathered garbage and tried mopping up the pools of liquor, but not before much of it had soaked into the porous hardwood floors. We tried to straighten the old lampshade before turning out the lights, locking the door and pulling away. As I looked back, I hoped the odorous thaw would dissipate undetected long before Memere and her girls arrived in early June for their summer break.

In years that followed I realized from listening to family dinner conversations that I was not the only one to sneak out to Petersfield for a bit of diversion. Victor, Phil and my brother Andre had their share of parties in the old insilbrick house, causing far more attention than I ever did. Word was slipped about a stout minded fellow named George who was discovered early one morning dancing naked on the dock, waving in white gulls after a late night soiree of beans and beer supplied by cousin Phil. And we mustn't forget the time when Uncle Toto brought two old fellows to Petersfield from the hotel to help with the spring clean up. They lost the use of their legs and most of their faculties after drinking skunky beer, long left behind by Camille after one of his little jaunts to Petersfield for a breath of fresh country air.

I learned a couple of things those frosty days in Petersfield. I learned that, old flame's kisses may not be as enjoyable as one may think, beer eventually goes bad and ancient hardwood floors soak up more than just atmosphere.

Most importantly, I learned you can do as many stupid things as you want when you are young, it is expected of you and most often tolerated.

# A PAINLESS FAREWELL

Despite my absence, summers with Memere carried on through the next few years. Memere and her girls let go of the second generation and made room for the third. Victor's son was born, bringing to mind vacations past as his mother was coerced into taking him to Petersfield for his summers with Memere. Faded dolphins frolicking in rigid, painted waves were depicted on the old plastic swimming pool that was resurrected and filled with creek water in early mornings to warm in the mounting, country sun. The three matriarchs, leaving his mother with little to do but enjoy the idleness afforded her, heaped hours of feminine attention upon this little lad. Stuffed with sweet edibles, he was taken for long walks down the dusty little back roads and his eyes were gently opened to the history of the beauty that surrounded him.

The first Sunday in August celebrations of Memere's birthday would carry on at Petersfield until 1976. On those occasions, I'd find myself wandering the perimeter of the property, searching for clues of the happy times that were summers past. After indulging in ripe red and yellow plums from gnarled, thorny trees in the orchard I would peer into the murky green creek, hoping to catch a glimpse of wiggly mud-pouts casting black shadows along the ragged, reedy shoreline. Only a big area of patchy weeds remained where the mysterious old barn once stood, it having been demolished in a swoop by ropes tied to Andre's car bumper one colourful, fall afternoon. A large garage was built behind the outhouse, to replace the barn and housed the things it once sheltered, articles such as Memere's lawn mower collection and the two big canoes. The structure was painted "barn red", maybe in an unintentional attempt to remind us of the days gone by.

One Armistice Day was the scene of a cool gathering at the old insilbrick house. A dusting of snow covered the floor of the orchard and withering lawn, prompting the building of a roaring fire in the blackened wood stove which stood boldly in one corner of the kitchen. The younger generation boasted about personal achievements while listening to music in the living room, leaving the older arthritic ones to sit in the kitchen, all bunched around the oil-clothed table, gleaning heat from each other. Not having proved to be the most pleasant time of the year to visit our Petersfield summer place, the fall celebration was not to be repeated.

After Memere's passing, everyone moved on in his or her individual directions. My summers were spent working to pay for the exotic winter vacations that would replace holidays at Petersfield. Employed by a national airline, my efforts were rewarded with passes to the world. Seldom did I look back. The old insilbrick house was packed away in a corner of my mind that was home to mostly hidden memories. Memories that would mean little to me until now when I realize how the experiences of my youth helped to sculpt my basic personality, values, love of country and deep family roots.

The years have tumbled by and somewhere along the way, we have all been visited by the "Long in the Tooth" fairy who has succeeded in pulling some of the colour from our hair, thickened our waists and introduced a little sag to our bottoms. Time has stolen some of our lives, leaving the rest of us to depend on old snap-shots and incidents that spark remembrance. Dad, Memere, Uncle Tommy, Auntie Emma, Auntie Lil and Nick have all passed away. We children survived our teenaged years and went on to work in various careers. Retirement is coming fast upon all of us, although not soon enough for some.

Mother is now looked upon as the matriarch of our family. She sold the empty lot at Winnipeg Beach and her share of Petersfield last year. It is difficult to pass nostalgic places on to someone else, to strangers, but the time comes to most of us sooner or later.

The Rube and I have renewed acquaintances and sometime since those Petersfield days, he lost his signature silver tooth to one of white enamel. I have regretfully, lost track of Alma but I know that Linda, who is now a grandmother, eventually settled in a little beach town just past Petersfield. Sadly, Donny, Garnet Walters, Hatchy and our two Elvis impersonators have "left the building".

My brother Andre is an electrical engineer working with communications and was transferred to an office in Edmonton four years ago. He decided he didn't want to live there before he left, but was given no choice. He claims as long as he gets his hair cut in Winnipeg, he hasn't really left.

While in town during September 1999, Andre decided, one clear brilliant day, to take Mother and I out on highway number nine to visit our old friend, Petersfield. We remarked on how it had been years since we travelled this road as the city stretched out before us to poke fingers of housed streets at which once were small hamlets. Stores and malls have replaced market farms and the old, North Main drive-in "passion pit". Many warm dark summer hours were spent at that drive-in, eating popcorn and

165

watching James Bond beat all the bad guys and win the hearts of beautiful women. In our early twenties, Hatchie and I would stop there Sunday nights on the way home from Winnipeg Beach. It was a social event, people car-hopping and hanging out in the concession stand, feasting on hot dogs and buttered popcorn. Every young person in town was there it seemed, and everyone knew everyone.

On this particular fall day, Andre stopped the car at Clandeboye, the small town just about five miles before Petersfield. Mom reminisced how we used to pause there for rainbow ice-cream cones and were pleased to find there was still a store with an adjoining restaurant boasting home-made fries, hot-dogs and ice cream but alas, no rainbow cones. We settled for strawberry, but it wasn't the same.

As we approached Petersfield there was a gathering of hunters just outside the Petersfield Motor Hotel. The men were dressed in camouflage, standing around a sport utility vehicle, which was draped with strings of lifeless geese and ducks. The sight reminded me of the old water-stained hunting pictures that hung in black frames on Pepere's walls.

A huge mallard duck, frozen in flight atop a pillar on the west side of the bridge smiled in our direction as we turned off the highway onto Edith road. All the streets have names now. We passed by the new Catholic Church on the corner as Mom craned her neck in vain, trying to catch a glimpse of the small simple white structure in which we spent warm sticky hours on those Sunday mornings, so many years ago. A monument now stands in its place.

Turning right onto Tommy Prince road, the car wound around the familiar bend with its wonderful view of the sparkling creek, its shores choked with bull-rushes and mossy weeds. Many a car has missed this turn on foggy nights or because of carelessness. The steep sloped bank has not claimed any lives that I can recall but has been the temporary parking lot for many a liquor-fuelled jalopy. We continued down the road past what was onceTrossi's turkey farm on the corner, now home only to hay bales and rusting farm machinery. Tiny cabins painted a variety of bright colours came into view, blinking through the bushes and aspen trees along the right side of the dusty gavel road. The small dwellings were situated very close together on the postage stamp sized lots littered with smoking barbeques, horseshoe pitches, lawn chairs and patio lanterns. Chelsey's old store, parking lot and tollbooth were still there, as if frozen in time like welcoming old friends. I have been told that the store and clubroom with its jukebox and fine old memories were burned to nothing sometime later and have been replaced by a modern new building.

We turned left, down the most familiar part of the stony, pot-holed road and approached with anticipation what' in our minds, should have been familiar but wasn't. Replacing the old gate with it's "OROY" sign, was a big 244 nailed to one of the ancestral trees, one of Pepere's old residents. We sat idling on the approach to the driveway for a few minutes contemplating entering the yard but decided to move on to Gilbert's, which again has a new name. The once long shady lane, which entered into the property, was now choked with trailers and tents, bunched together like so many little boxes topped with antennas and awnings.

Andre manoeuvred the van, squeezed for space in the lane and turned back toward Chesley's, stopping at our old driveway for one last look. All the trees were still there, even the twisted old plum and apple trees in the orchard. The new owner was even careful to preserve the Virginia creeper that Auntie Lil planted to camouflage our little green out-house, which still stood beside the red garage.

We decided to turn into the yard and down the drive to where the old rusty-coloured insilbrick structure once stood.

There was emptiness, the foundation lying silent, buried below the muddy surface. Beside the empty plot had risen a modern new home with vinyl siding and a beautiful expanse of glass facing Netley Creek. There was a sunroom to catch the Southern sunshine and the back, almost windowless against the imminent winter winds. The Impressive structure sat high on a concrete pedestal to guard against flooding and when I knocked, the door opened to gleaming hardwood floors and a small white dog. The new owner invited us to view the property at our leisure, but it only took a few minutes to satisfy our minds and hearts.

The front yard still held a breathtaking sight of the creek offering its treasures of leisure activities. The banks are now heavily populated with expansive dwellings, boathouses and there was a pontoon plane bobbing in the water directly across from us.

As we turned to leave, Mom tamped the ground with her foot atop the spot where the old house once stood as if trying to feel its presence.

We left that day, knowing we would probably not return. Petersfield has moved on, growing and stretching, leaving us buried in its past. We will also continue to move ahead to other things, making new memories and cherishing the old, the ones that will sleep deep within our hearts and smile to us from old photo albums.

The last time I was in Petersfield, I learned that it could sometimes bring heartbreak to see what has become of the past. Beautiful places are sought after by the human heart and change and grow with the parade of ages. I want to believe this is why God instilled in each of us the gift of memory, a priceless tool to help us slip back to the places of years ago. All those special places where we can relive the good times and savour our own personal histories, whenever we please.

Printed in the United States
By Bookmasters